THE HUMAN EQUATION

PENTA FACTOR

"LEADING WITH HEART"
A GUIDE TO BUILDING
PEOPLE-FIRST ORGANISATIONS

DEVAPRASAD DEVDAS

INDIA • SINGAPORE • MALAYSIA

Copyright © Devaprasad Devdas 2024
All Rights Reserved.

ISBN 979-8-89498-800-9

This book has been published with all efforts taken to make the material error-free after the consent of the author. However, the author and the publisher do not assume and hereby disclaim any liability to any party for any loss, damage, or disruption caused by errors or omissions, whether such errors or omissions result from negligence, accident, or any other cause.

While every effort has been made to avoid any mistake or omission, this publication is being sold on the condition and understanding that neither the author nor the publishers or printers would be liable in any manner to any person by reason of any mistake or omission in this publication or for any action taken or omitted to be taken or advice rendered or accepted on the basis of this work. For any defect in printing or binding the publishers will be liable only to replace the defective copy by another copy of this work then available.

Contents

Acknowledgement

Writing this book has been a transformative journey, and it would not have been possible without the incredible support of so many. First and foremost, a deep thank you to the universe, the guiding force that brought this project to life.

To my teachers and all my mentors, your wisdom and guidance laid the foundation for this work. My friends and colleagues, your encouragement and camaraderie, fuelled my passion throughout the process. And to the experiences – both joyful and tearful – you have shaped my perspective and enriched this book's content.

A special dedication goes to my family. Your unwavering support provided the wind beneath my wings, allowing this book to take flight. I would not be here without you.

This book is also for everyone I have encountered on life's path. Each interaction, big or small, has played a role in shaping my thoughts and ultimately contributing to this work. Among these influences, a heartfelt thank you to my teacher, Pramila. Your kindness and guidance were instrumental in nurturing my abilities and fostering my confidence. May you rest in peace, and may your spirit continue to inspire others to reach for the skies.

Finally, this book is dedicated to every child and dreamer out there. No matter how challenging the path may seem, never let go of your dreams. Hold onto your faith, and remember, anything is possible.

With heartfelt gratitude,

Dev

Preface

Have you ever wondered what truly makes a workplace thrive? It is a question that lingers in the minds of many. We often get caught up in complex structures and processes, forgetting the most crucial element – the human beings who make it all function.

This book takes a refreshingly simple approach: it views the workplace through a human lens. Forget the idea of ourselves as separate from our colleagues or the organisation itself. The truth is, we are all part of the equation. Our efforts, big or small, have the power to shape the environment we work in.

But let us face it, a workplace is a melting pot. We come together with diverse perspectives, emotions, needs, and, yes, even conflicts. Striving for universal happiness might be a beautiful idea, but it is an impossible one. However, what we can achieve is a sense of collective satisfaction, where each individual feels valued and empowered to contribute.

Here is where the human element takes centre stage. It is the collective needs, expectations, and even egos of individuals that create the unique culture of an organisation. This culture, in turn, plays a critical role in shaping success.

This book explores the core factors that build a morally sound and successful, people-centric organisation. We will explore how leaders and individuals alike possess the power to transform their workplaces. We will shed light on the essential dynamics that make a human-centric approach:

- ***The Dynamics of Hierarchy***: Exploring the structure of organisations, uncovering the benefits, and challenges of hierarchies in a people-centric environment.

- ***The Power of Openness***: Cultivating transparency and understanding why open communication is vital for a healthy workplace.

- ***Integrity in Action***: Aligning actions with words for organisational integrity, because walking the talk truly matters.

- ***Fair Rewards and Earned Recognition***: Building a fair system for rewards and recognition, ensuring transparency in how contributions are valued.

- ***Support as Investment***: Empowering employees by viewing support as a strategic investment that fuels motivation and success.

- ***The Penta Factor***: Building on these core dynamics to create a solid foundation for a people-centric organisation.

Throughout this journey, we will expose the elements that must not be ignored – from designing organisations and crafting policies, to establishing workflows and fostering a positive culture. In short, we will explore every facet of the organisational life cycle through a human lens.

This book is for anyone who, like you, are a curious human seeking answers and striving to make a positive impact. It is for those who believe in the power of creating a better place to work. By combining my experience as a human resource professional with insightful research, we will embark on a journey to explore the most well-known yet often overlooked element – the human element.

Are you ready to unlock the potential of a people-centric organisation?

Together, let us turn the dream of a "better place" into a reality.

Let us begin!

Introduction

The whirring gears and flashing lights of Artificial Intelligence (AI) paint a picture of a future transformed. Headlines scream about job displacement – self-driving cars replacing taxi drivers, algorithms writing marketing copy, and robots assembling products on factory lines. These advancements raise a profound question: ***Will our jobs be taken over by machines?***

While some tasks will undoubtedly become automated, the answer is not a simple one. Yes, there will be job losses, but a fascinating shift is also occurring. Traditional job descriptions are dissolving, replaced by a mosaic of in-demand skills. The future workforce will not be defined by titles, but by the expertise or the skill of individuals possess.

The Human Spark: Beyond Replication

In this era of rapid change, it is vital to remember that the human brain, the very source of AI, holds an unparalleled power. We are the architects of these technological marvels, and our natural intelligence will continue to drive innovation.

Machines may be replicating some human tasks, but the skills needed to navigate this evolving landscape – creativity, critical thinking, and social intelligence – remain irreplaceable for now.

Survival of the Fittest: Attracting the Creative Minds

In this new world order, organisations that thrive will not just focus on skills acquisition. They will cultivate an environment that unlocks human potential. This is because, only a highly skilled human can cultivate and drive changes. As mentioned earlier, it is the human brain that is propelling technology.

We must recognise the crucial truth: in an age of automation, human skills are the new gold. These rare talents are not just a "nice to have" – they are essential for survival. But attracting this talent is just the first hurdle. The real challenge lies in retaining them, nurturing their skills, and fostering a loyalty that transcends the traditional employee-employer relationship.

In today's landscape, success is not just about having competent employees; it is about attracting and retaining those with exceptional, creative minds. With the rise of technology, the world is shrinking. Employee experiences become public knowledge, instantly shared and evaluated. Organisations with positive, human-centric cultures will attract the best talent, while those lacking in these core values will struggle to survive.

This is where the **Penta Factor** comes in – a framework that goes beyond traditional management practices to address our fundamental human needs. The five factors, which are not new – **Hierarchy, Openness, Integrity, Reward and Recognition**, and **Support** – are the cornerstones of a successful and harmonious organisation.

Imagine a hierarchy less about rigid structures and more about fostering a culture of innovation, where every voice is heard. Combine this with an environment of **openness**, built on transparency and trust, and you have a foundation for collaboration and integrity. Add a system of **reward and recognition** that acknowledges valuable contributions, and a robust **Support** network that caters to employee well-being, and you have the recipe for a passionate, motivated workforce.

The Penta Factor does not just improve organisational success – it fuels a positive and ethical work culture. It recognises the human need for belonging, respect, and purpose, all of which translate into a powerful force that drives positive judgement and fosters strong group values.

Throughout this book, we will examine more deeply into each aspect of the Penta Factor, exploring how these core elements can be utilised to create an environment where humans can flourish.

Retaining talent is not solely an HR function; it is a business imperative. It strengthens organisational synergy, improves brand value, and showcases genuine commitment to our people. It demonstrates that the organisation values human connection and understands the need to earn employee acceptance – a crucial factor for a world saturated with AI and automation.

A Human Experience

Throughout this book, we will investigate the human experience within an organisation. We will not look at it through the lens of an HR professional, a board member, or a CEO – we will examine it through a human lens. This perspective allows us to understand and validate the factors that truly impact employees' emotions and, ultimately, their judgement of the organisation.

We will discuss the five core factors – **Hierarchy, Openness, Integrity, Reward and Recognition, and Support** – which are constantly evaluated by the individuals who make up the organisation. These elements become the deciding factors for employee sentiment, impacting the overall experience and, ultimately, their decision to 'stay' or to 'go.'

We will dissect the traditional hierarchy, uncovering how it can unwittingly stifle creativity. We will investigate into the cracks of a closed culture, uncovering the factors that prevent open communication. We will shine a light on the disconnect between words and actions, a surefire way to erode trust.

Loyalty, once a cornerstone of the workplace, has become a rare gem. We will explore why, and more importantly, how to cultivate it. The imbalance in reward and recognition systems will be brought to light, revealing its detrimental effects. And we will unveil the magic a well-crafted support system can unleash.

By putting on our human hats, stepping back to observe, and analysing these core elements, we will uncover the secrets behind employee judgement and the spark that ignites passion.

By stripping away the layers and observing these elements through a human lens, we will uncover the hidden triggers that shape employee judgement and ignite the passion that fuels success.

At the end of every chapter, we will dive into the mind of an egotistical leader, where thoughts and intentions are fuelled by pure ego and self-superiority. This humorous exploration features an imaginary leader – it could be me or anyone else – who reveals their egocentric musings. Expect to spill the beans on their grandiose self-image, offering you a chance to smile and reflect. This tongue-in-cheek look at leadership will provide both laughs and insights, making you ponder the quirks of those who believe they are always the smartest person in the room. Enjoy the ride as we uncover the hilarity behind the ego!

So, are you ready to begin this journey? Let us unlock the human potential within your organisation, together.

Chapter 1

The Dynamics of Hierarchy

Throughout history, human societies have established structures to organise and distribute power. This often took the form of hierarchies, with clear leadership at the top and varying levels of authority below. While hierarchies once brought stability and clear lines of responsibility, they can also breed limitations.

While these hierarchical structures are ingrained in every aspect of society, from national governments to local communities and even business organisations, within these hierarchies, a common belief holds sway: the higher one sits in the pyramid, the more valid their decisions.

This is reflected in the proverb "the boss is always right," reinforcing the expectation that subordinates should unquestionably accept the decisions of their superiors.

This blind acceptance of hierarchy comes with a cost. It fosters a culture of fear – fear of questioning authority, fear of accountability, fear of being ostracised for proposing "dumb ideas," and fear of being perceived as arrogant for suggesting alternative solutions.

Ultimately, the validity of these hierarchical systems rests on a foundation of fear, not on the merits of the ideas themselves.

This chapter explores the concept of hierarchy, not to dismantle it, but to challenge its traditional dominance. We will examine the limitations of rigid hierarchies and the bureaucracy and explore alternative models that empower knowledge and innovation at all levels.

Before we embark on this journey, let us ask a fundamental question: What constitutes the ideal leadership model?

Is it the lone visionary, charting a course with unwavering conviction? Or perhaps a dynamic team, brimming with diverse perspectives and innovative ideas? Alternatively, should we prioritize a structured system designed to minimize errors and self-interest? Perhaps the answer lies in a simpler approach – i.e., nurturing a team united by trust and a shared purpose.

The reality is creative solutions often emerge from a collaborative environment. When a diverse team with a common goal works together, they can generate a wider range of ideas, fostering innovation and problem-solving.

A 2021 Deloitte study of Fortune 500 companies[9] revealed a striking correlation: organizations with diverse leadership teams outperformed their less diverse counterparts by a substantial 35% in profitability.

The story of Kodak, despite having invented the digital camera in the 1970s, Kodak failed to recognise its potential, ultimately ceding the market to more adaptable competitors[11]. All of this suggests that a wider range of perspectives leads to better decision-making and innovation, and even great ideas championed by visionary leaders can falter in the absence of a strong team.

Now, imagine a scenario where multiple, equally strong solutions are presented. What truly separates the best team leader from the rest?

It is the adaptability and willingness to embrace the most suitable solution, regardless of its source. This leader does not just generate ideas; they facilitate open communication, guide the team towards the best solution, and ensure everyone feels comfortable contributing.

Wright Brothers, credited with the first successful controlled flight. While Orville is often seen as the "leader" of the duo, their success stemmed from a collaborative effort where Wilbur's theoretical knowledge and piloting skills complemented Orville's mechanical expertise[10]. This synergy between diverse skill sets is a hallmark of successful teams.

This chapter explores the limitations of the "lone genius" and discusses the power of fostering a collaborative environment. We will examine how effective leadership empowers teams to generate diverse ideas, fosters open communication, and, ultimately, selects the best course of action for achieving the common goal.

Houston, We Have a Problem: A Tale of Two Worlds [12]

Imagine hurtling towards the moon, a million miles from home, when your spaceship suffers a catastrophic explosion. This was not science fiction; it was the terrifying reality faced by the Apollo 13 crew in 1970. Their mission, a triumphant lunar landing, was thrown into chaos as their oxygen tank blew, crippling the spacecraft and leaving them with limited power and dwindling life support.

Back on Earth, a different kind of panic gripped Mission Control. Gene Kranz, the steely-eyed flight director, knew the clock was ticking. Saving the astronauts would not be a one-man show. He assembled a unique team – a diverse group of engineers, each with their own specialty.

Veteran engineers brought years of experience, while younger minds offered fresh perspectives. It was a delicate dance. Kranz needed to harness their collective knowledge while ensuring clear direction.

The situation demanded a meeting of the minds. Imagine the scene: a room buzzing with nervous energy, as ideas flew back and forth. One engineer proposed a radical solution – using components from the Lunar Module, originally meant for a short lunar stay, to create a makeshift filtration system for the crippled Command Module.

This was not a conventional approach, but desperation breeds innovation. The team's diverse expertise proved vital. The "space plumbers," as they were sometimes called, meticulously planned the procedure, translating complex engineering concepts into clear instructions for the astronauts. Every hose, every adapter, every filter, mattered. There was no room for error.

Meanwhile, aboard Apollo 13, the crew faced a different kind of battle. With limited resources and a jury-rigged system hanging by a thread, they had to trust the engineers on Earth and their own skills. Imagine the constant hum of the makeshift system, a fragile lifeline keeping them alive. Every passing minute was a testament to human courage and ingenuity.

The effort paid off. The astronauts successfully re-entered Earth's atmosphere, splashing down in the Pacific Ocean to a hero's welcome. The world watched in awe, relief washing over them, as the battered spacecraft returned home.

The Apollo 13 mission was not just about flawless technology or daring astronauts; it was a story of collaboration. Kranz's leadership, the diverse expertise of the engineers, and the unwavering spirit of the crew – all these elements played a critical role in turning disaster into triumph.

Throughout a workday, ideas, suggestions, and recommendations flow freely between colleagues. However, resistance can arise from two sources: 'Individual' and 'Environmental.'

On the individual level, people may hesitate to share their best ideas due to fear of rejection or a lack of confidence. The environment can also play a role, with hurdles like bureaucracy, approval processes, and workplace politics, hindering the flow of information.

Here, leaders play a crucial role in fostering a culture that encourages the exchange of insights. By promoting open communication, collaboration, and a focus on the bigger picture, they can create an environment where everyone feels comfortable sharing their ideas.

While departmental structures can improve efficiency, working in isolation and neglecting collective goals can stifle creativity and mutual support. It is important to strike a balance. When departments become overly focused on their own objectives, they can lose sight of the broader organisational goals.

The key takeaway is that organisations are made up of interconnected parts. Departments, processes, teams, and individuals all contribute to the whole. By encouraging collaboration and open communication across all levels, organisations can unleash the power of collective thinking.

While, in most cases, hierarchy becomes a hurdle and takes away a lot of potential opportunities and solutions to the problem.

We might have experienced a situation where the suggestion from a stranger or a lesser known, no matter how brilliant it would be, there will be a pitch of scepticism.

In real life, this applies to the similar voices in the boardroom. We feel confident in the ideas from the one we know, from the one in my team, or from the one we are familiar with, as we are sure of their past records and achievements.

In boardrooms (and everyday situations), we often place more trust in ideas presented by those we know well, like colleagues or team members. This "familiarity bias" stems from a sense of comfort based on past performance and established relationships.

Here, the Apollo 13 mission becomes a powerful reminder of the importance of fostering environments where diverse voices are heard and where leadership guides collaboration towards a shared goal. In the face of seemingly insurmountable odds, the "Balancing Act" of leadership and diverse input can lead to extraordinary outcomes.

We all revere the iconic leaders whose stories ignite our imaginations, but let us step away from the spotlight for a moment.

What about the culture and platform that nurtured these leaders? This begs the question: who creates whom?

"Is it the great leader who builds a great team, or is it the exceptional team that elevates a leader?"

The answer, like most things in life, is not so black and white. It is a beautiful symphony of interdependence. A leader cannot exist in a vacuum, and a team, without a guiding force, often struggles to reach its full potential.

Leaders who choose to work alongside their teams, sharing their knowledge, and actively encouraging participation, exhibit the hallmarks of potentially great leaders. This approach embodies the philosophy of "Leaders create leaders, not just followers."

By fostering a space where leadership skills can be nurtured and developed within the team itself, this leadership style goes beyond simply managing followers. It recognises that the collective wisdom of the team surpasses the knowledge of any single individual.

This collaborative approach has several benefits. By sharing knowledge and encouraging participation, leaders empower team members to take ownership, think critically, and develop their leadership potential. This creates a synergy where the sum becomes greater than its parts, leading to a more innovative and successful team.

The truth is a hierarchical wall that supposedly separates leaders from their teams.

Effective leadership thrives in environments were communication flows freely, regardless of position. Similarly, departmental silos that hinder collaboration are another enemy to be conquered.

While we establish the importance of fostering leadership alongside team development, a crucial question remains: **what hinders the flow of ideas?**

When a team member proposes an idea, it often faces roadblocks before gaining acceptance.

In the next section, we will explore deeper by examining this concept through the lens of a "**Flow of creativity**" with the help of a graph. This can help us illustrate the typical hurdles encountered during the flow of ideas within an organisation.

Furthermore, we will explore how organisations can actively cultivate an environment that embraces the free flow of ideas.

Flow of Creativity

Imagine the birth of a brilliant idea as a small spark in the vast landscape of an individual's mind. This spark, full of potential and promise, embarks on a journey filled with challenges and triumphs before it reaches its ultimate goal: acceptance and implementation within the organisation.

Imagine a brilliant idea as a tiny seed bursting forth from the fertile ground of our imagination. This ground represents our 'Self', enriched by our unique experiences, beliefs, and knowledge. This is the spark, the initial stage of idea generation and self-validation. We nurture this seed with enthusiasm, assessing its potential and feasibility.

But soon, a weed pokes through the soil – the fear of presentation. Will our idea be ridiculed? Will it be deemed worthless? These anxieties threaten to choke the life out of our fledgling idea.

Here, the role of the environment comes into play. We seek a safe haven, a nurturing garden, to cultivate our idea. This might be a supportive colleague or mentor who provides valuable feedback and helps us conquer our fears.

Perhaps it's a brainstorming session or a team meeting where our idea can blossom under the scrutiny of others. This collaborative environment allows our idea to grow and adapt, receiving sunlight and water from diverse perspectives.

Through this process of refinement, our idea gains strength and resilience. Now, it is ready to face the final hurdle: the decision-makers. This powerful force of nature, like a scorching sun or a heavy rain, can either nourish our idea or wither it away. But with the backing of our supportive environment and our own unwavering belief, our idea can persevere and reach its full potential.

Influencers	Self		Environment		
Dynamics	Getting Idea & Self Validation	Fear of Presentation	Platform to present	Group Acceptance	Approval for the Idea

The "Flow of Creativity" chart maps out this fascinating journey through four pivotal stages, highlighting the influences and dynamics that shape the path of innovation.

Creativity or the flow of ideas is influenced by two main factors, which are *'Self' and 'Environment.'*

Self: These encompass our individual beliefs, understandings, and anything within our personal control. They act as the foundation for our ideas, driving the initial spark and nurturing it through the preliminary stages of development.

Environment: These represent external factors that influence us, such as societal expectations, situational pressures, and anything beyond our individual control. The environment can either hinder or facilitate the progression of an idea from conception to realisation.

The Stages of Idea Generation

Let the journey of an idea be broken down into five distinct stages, each influenced by both self and environmental dynamics:

Stage 1: Idea Generation and Self-Validation *(Self - Internal Dynamics)*

Getting the Idea and Self-Validation: Every great innovation starts with a moment of inspiration. At this initial stage, an individual conceives an idea, a unique solution to a problem, or an improvement to an existing process.

The individual grapples with self-validation, assessing the feasibility and potential impact of their idea. This phase is characterised by excitement and introspection, as the innovator builds confidence in their concept. Convincing ourselves of our idea's merit is essential before moving forward.

Stage 2: Overcoming Fear, *(Self - Internal and External Dynamics)*

Fear of Presentation: As the idea takes shape, the next hurdle emerges – the fear of presentation. The innovator faces self-doubt and apprehension about sharing their idea with others.

Questions arise: Will it be well received? Is it truly valuable?

These anxieties might include fear of failure, questioning by authority figures, accountability, being ostracised for seemingly "dumb" ideas, or being perceived as arrogant for suggesting alternative solutions.

Overcoming this fear is crucial for the idea to move forward, requiring courage and self-assurance.

Internally, confidence can be developed through thorough preparation and rehearsal. Externally, seeking support from a trusted group (colleagues, mentors, or friends) can provide valuable feedback and help quell presentation anxieties.

Stage 3: Securing the Right Platform (*Self and Environment - Collaborative Dynamics*)

Platform to Present: Once the fear is conquered, the innovator seeks a platform to present their idea. This stage is a collaborative effort influenced by both self and environmental dynamics.

Finding the right platform requires initiative on the part of the innovator.

However, a supportive group plays a crucial role in creating opportunities for an individual to showcase their ideas. It could be a team meeting, a brainstorming session, or a formal proposal.

The platform acts as a bridge, transforming a solitary idea into a shared vision.

Stage 4: Group Acceptance and Refinement (*Environment - Internal Dynamics*)

Group Acceptance: The idea enters a collaborative environment where it encounters the perspectives and critiques of a broader group.

This stage is marked by rigorous discussions, feedback, and modifications. Presenting the idea to a group fosters discussion, challenges assumptions, and helps identify potential weaknesses.

Group acceptance is essential for the idea to gain traction. Here, the innovator navigates through varying opinions, building consensus and refining the idea to align with collective goals.

This collaborative brainstorming strengthens the idea and increases its chances of success.

Stage 5: Idea Approval (*Environment - External Dynamics*)

Approval for the Idea: Finally, the idea reaches the decision-makers who have the authority to implement it. This stage involves formal evaluation, resource allocation, and strategic alignment.

Approval signifies the culmination of the idea's journey from a spark of inspiration to a concrete plan, ready for execution.

Following group acceptance, the final decision to move forward with the idea rests on factors beyond our immediate control. However, the group, including the innovator, can influence the decision-makers and gain crucial approval.

The Importance of Balance

With the help of the '**Flow of Creativity**,' we can illuminate the pivotal role of self-belief and support mechanisms in the creative process. At the outset, an individual must have unwavering confidence in themselves and their idea. Access to resources is equally essential, enabling them to refine and present their concepts effectively.

The journey of creativity is a delicate dance between personal initiative and collective validation. Each stage of this journey represents a critical phase where ideas must evolve, confronting both internal doubts and external scrutiny.

Understanding this flow is vital for organisations striving to cultivate a supportive environment that nurtures innovation. Encouraging employees to voice their most innovative ideas, and ensuring those ideas receive the attention they deserve, can significantly enhance an organisation's creative output.

By recognising and addressing the challenges at each stage of the creative process, both individuals and organisations can foster a culture rich in creativity and continuous improvement. This approach not only promotes sustainable success, but also drives ongoing growth and development. Embracing this dynamic can lead to a more vibrant, innovative, and resilient organisation, where creativity thrives and propels the entire enterprise forward.

By acknowledging and addressing the hurdles at each stage, both individuals and organisations can foster a culture of creativity and continuous improvement, leading to sustainable success and growth.

Resistance to innovative ideas often stems from individual anxieties about presenting, gaining acceptance, or facing potential challenges.

These anxieties can be amplified by ingrained biases like **"familiarity bias"** or the **"my-team-is-best"** mentality in the leadership team, which further creates a siloed approach within the organisation.

Here comes the role of effective leaders who foster an environment that transcends hierarchy and prioritises collective goals. To cultivate a culture of open innovation, leaders must embrace ideas from all corners of the organisation, not just their inner circle.

While a leader's experience is valuable for anticipating obstacles, they should avoid stifling creativity with bureaucratic hurdles or the assumption that "the boss is always right."

The Trap of Solipsism

Imagine a high-wire act. A skilled performer strides across a taut rope, seemingly defying gravity. But maintaining that balance requires constant adjustments, a keen awareness of their body, and a focus on the destination. Leadership operates in a similar space.

A well-defined hierarchy forms the sturdy rope, providing structure, clear roles and a sense of direction. This framework is essential for navigating any complex organisation.

But a rigid hierarchy can also morph into a tightrope walker's nightmare – a restrictive cage that fosters a dangerous mindset: **'Solipsism.'**

Solipsism is a psychological trap where an individual becomes convinced that their perspective is the only one that matters. Like an echo chamber, they are surrounded by their own ideas, often dismissing or minimising the views of others.

This can manifest in several detrimental ways:

- The "My Way or the Highway" Approach: Leaders or decision-makers bulldoze through decisions, disregarding valuable insights from team members.

- Innovation Graveyard: Fearful of change, leadership clings to traditional methods, stifling innovation, and the exploration of new ideas.

- Communication Breakdown: A one-way street of communication develops where only the leader's voice is heard, hindering collaboration and trust.

The consequences of solipsism are dire. Team members feel disengaged, creativity dries up, and the organisation becomes stagnant, unable to adapt to changing realities.

Recognising and overcoming solipsistic tendencies is a crucial step towards becoming a more effective leader. By actively seeking and valuing diverse perspectives, leaders can foster a more inclusive and innovative environment. Encouraging open communication and embracing change, not only empowers team members, but also ensures the organisation remains dynamic and resilient in the face of evolving challenges.

In summary, breaking free from the confines of solipsism can rejuvenate an organisation, unleashing a wave of creativity and engagement that drives long-term success and adaptability.

Imagine ourselves trapped within a room lined entirely with mirrors. Our voices echo back, our thoughts amplified. This is the essence of solipsism—the belief that only our own minds and experiences are real. As leaders, it is easy for us to get caught in this echo chamber, surrounded by yes-men, or simply consumed by our own ideas. ***Fortunately, there is a path for us to break free and build a truly connected team***.

The first step is to crack open a window. We can cultivate *self-awareness* by reflecting on our interactions. Do we dismiss others' perspectives? Do our opinions dominate the conversation? Recognising these tendencies is the first step towards bridging the gap.

Next, let us step outside the chamber entirely. We should *seek feedback*. We should not just surround ourselves with people who agree with us. Actively soliciting honest assessments from team members, peers, and mentors is crucial. Constructive criticism, though it might sting initially, can be a powerful tool for our growth.

Empathy becomes our bridge to others. We must make a conscious effort to understand their experiences and perspectives. Actively listening, even when viewpoints differ, strengthens our connections and makes our work environment more inclusive and thriving.

Let us embrace the cacophony! Recognising the value of ***diverse thought*** is vital. We should not just seek out input from those who echo our own ideas. Actively seeking out divergent backgrounds, experiences, and expertise enriches our team. Creating opportunities for open dialogue and collaboration, where alternative viewpoints are not just heard but celebrated, is essential.

We need to ***delegate*** and trust. We do not have to be the hero in every story. By empowering our team members through delegating tasks and trusting them to excel, we recognise that collaboration, not solo acts, leads to true success.

We should ***challenge our own assumptions***. Our initial ideas are not always gospel. Being open to new perspectives, even if they shake our existing beliefs, is crucial. Continuous learning is key to dismantling the walls of solipsism. As leaders, we must commit to ongoing learning through books, workshops, or leadership training programmes. By embracing lifelong learning, we become beacons for our team, guiding them out of their own echo chambers and into a world of collaboration and success.

The ideal leader, like a skilled tightrope walker, masters the art of balance. They understand the value of their own experience and perspective while recognising the importance of incorporating diverse voices.

Seeking feedback is crucial for refining ideas and avoiding the solipsism trap.

Leadership as a Filter, not a Dam

While hierarchy and an organised system are essential for many reasons, they establish accountability and can provide guidance and leadership in a structured environment. Without an organisational matrix, it will be a challenging task to find rhythm and properly implement the policies and follow procedures.

While democratic principles ensure everyone's voice is heard, in a practical setting, it can lead to diffused accountability and decision fatigue. As the saying goes, "Too many cooks spoil the broth." Here, leadership steps in to find the sweet spot.

Effective leaders do not simply listen to diverse perspectives; they act as a filter, considering various experiences before making decisions. This involves not only acknowledging ideas, but also assessing their feasibility and potential challenges.

Through this process, they champion the most effective action plan for the benefit of the organisation.

A thriving organisation encourages a culture where diverse ideas are valued, and open communication allows for informed decision-making. However, leadership is not just about soliciting input; it is about making well-considered choices, setting direction, and guiding your team towards a shared goal.

By prioritising a collaborative environment while making responsible decisions, leaders can avoid the pitfalls of solipsism and guide their teams toward a path of success, innovation, and collective achievement.

We must recognise that the concept of hierarchy, not as a rigid structure, but as a necessary scaffold that supports organised business operations. *"A healthy hierarchy shouldn't translate into a mental hierarchy, where egos dictate the flow of ideas."*

Peering into an organisation, two key aspects often capture our attention: the structure, a map of who reports to whom, and the hierarchy, the pecking order that dictates information flow. While these elements are distinct, they play a crucial role in shaping an organisation's culture.

Earlier, we discussed the dangers of a rigid, "metal" hierarchy. It can become a roadblock, stifling the flow of creative ideas and suggestions. Imagine brilliant ideas struggling to navigate an approval chain filled with hurdles, their potential lost before they even reach the decision-makers.

When an organisation operates with a strong mental hierarchy, creativity gets stifled. This is why, as we build and develop an organisation, one of the key steps is to design a structure that empowers individuals without falling prey to hierarchical limitations. We can call this the "hierarchy trap."

There's no one-size-fits-all answer to building a structure that fosters creativity. It is not about rigid policies or restrictive frameworks. It is about fostering a shared understanding of the importance of structure while removing the shackles of hierarchy. We need a structure that appreciates and encourages creative expression within established boundaries.

We shall recognise hierarchy matrix not as a rigid ladder to be climbed, but as a network of interconnected platforms. Here, ideas can flow freely across levels, fuelled by mutual respect and a shared commitment to excellence.

It is in this space where hierarchy meets open-mindedness that innovation truly flourishes.

What Ego Whispers

Let us pause a moment and listen to ego.

"I have slaved away to get where I am, and my success practically screams, "I told you so!" Naturally, I demand respect. Those below me better listen up and learn. Seriously, think twice before spouting opinions. It is all about the seasoned solution, folks!"

As the fearless leader, I will gladly take the credit and steer us to victory. After all, someone has to take the reins, and who better than me? I mean, it is not bragging if it is true, right? Every step of the way, I have been the guiding light in this maze of chaos and confusion. Without my wisdom, who knows where we would be? Probably still figuring out how to turn the printer on.

But fear not, dear team, for I am here. With my unmatched expertise and dazzling charisma, we will conquer every challenge. So, heed my words, follow my lead, and remember: success has a name, and it's mine. Now, let us march towards victory – or, at least, towards the coffee machine for a much-needed break.

And if you need any more proof of my greatness, just ask me – I will be more than happy to tell you all about it."

Chapter 2

The Power of Openness

During our discussions on hierarchy and the mental traps that create barriers to creativity and disrupt innovation, one critical element emerged: the organisation and its people deeply desire a transparent, open culture. Such a culture not only fosters creativity but also breaks down the walls that stifle new ideas.

While it is clear that numerous factors influence decision-making, the power of openness consistently stands out. Organisations that embrace diverse perspectives, actively seek added information, and challenge existing assumptions, are better equipped to navigate the complexities of today's marketplace.

This openness not only enhances decision-making but also cultivates an environment where innovation thrives. By valuing transparency and encouraging open dialogue, companies can create a dynamic atmosphere that supports growth and adaptability.

Employees feel more engaged and empowered when their voices are heard, leading to increased collaboration and a shared sense of purpose. This inclusive approach enables organisations to respond more effectively to challenges and seize opportunities with agility and insight.

In summary, fostering an open culture is not just beneficial, but essential for organisations aiming to stay competitive and innovative. Embracing openness allows for a richer exchange of ideas, driving the organisation forward in an ever-changing business landscape.

Imagine a team where the leader calls the shots. If they fall prey to closed-mindedness or the "solipsism trap" (remember that from the previous chapter? That is the danger of clinging too tightly to our own wisdom, blind to the valuable insights of others), guess what? The entire group dynamic starts to reflect that same narrow way of thinking. It is like a domino effect – the leader's attitude tumbles down, shaping the team's culture.

There is an ancient Sanskrit proverb that perfectly captures this idea: **"Yadha Raja Thadha Prajah,"** which translates to *"As is the king, so are his people."* This wisdom applies far beyond royalty. In any group, from a corporate team to a social circle, the leader sets the tone. Their approach to decision-making, communication, and openness shapes how everyone else behaves.

Imagine a team where the leader throws open the doors to ideas, encourages healthy debate, and celebrates transparency. This is not just wishful thinking – it is a recipe for success. When a leader prioritises openness, fairness, and transparency, these values become embedded in the team's DNA. Everyone feels empowered to contribute, new ideas are met with excitement, and a spirit of trust takes root. It is like tossing a pebble into a still pond – the leader's actions create ripples of positive change that impact everyone.

On the other hand, a leader who operates in the shadows, shrouding themselves in secrecy, fosters a suffocating environment. Promising ideas get buried, innovation takes a backseat, and trust withers away. Think of it as a thick fog descending – communication gets muddled, misunderstandings multiply, and the team becomes paralysed by a lack of clarity.

Numerous studies across organisational behaviour, psychology, and leadership fields highlight the undeniable impact leaders have on their teams. We will discuss two key concepts: **Leader–Member Exchange Theory (LMX)** and **Communication Climate** [27, 28, 29, 30].

The **Leader–Member Exchange Theory (LMX)** posits that leaders develop unique relationships with each member of their team, and these relationships influence members' attitudes and behaviours. High-quality exchanges are associated with higher levels of trust, respect, and mutual obligation, which positively affect the team's overall performance and morale.

Adding to the **LMX theory**, **Communication Climate** discusses the way leaders communicate (e.g., openness, clarity, frequency) shapes the communication climate of the organisation. Leaders who promote open and transparent communication foster a culture of trust and collaboration, while poor communication from leaders can lead to misunderstandings and a lack of trust.

Leaders are the architects of culture. Whether through building strong relationships (LMX) or fostering open communication (climate), they have the power to set the stage for success. Just remember, hiding behind a veil of secrecy will not make things clearer – it will only cloud the path forward.

The bottom line? Creating a culture of openness, fairness, and transparency is not optional – it is essential. When leaders embrace these values, they empower their teams to reach their full potential.

The Enron Implosion[2]

Imagine a company, Enron, once a shining star in the energy industry. Its executives, like characters in a thrilling heist film, cooked the books. They hid mountains of debt, burying them deep within financial statements, a secret society of numbers only they could decipher. This web of deceit was not just a minor accounting error; it was a full-blown case of financial trickery.

For a while, the illusion held. Enron's stock price soared, investors cheered, and employees basked in a false sense of security. But the house of cards could not hold forever. When the truth came crashing down, it was a domino effect of devastation. The company, once a giant, declared bankruptcy, leaving a trail of wreckage in its wake.

Thousands of employees lost their jobs, their dreams of a secure future vanishing overnight. Pension plans, meant to provide a safety net in retirement, evaporated. Investors who had entrusted their hard-earned money to Enron watched in disbelief as their billions vanished into thin air.

The fallout did not stop there. Arthur Andersen, the prestigious accounting firm that had signed off on Enron's fraudulent statements, faced the consequences. Their reputation, built on trust and integrity, crumbled. The scandal led to their dissolution, a stark reminder that even the biggest names can fall from grace when they stray from the path of transparency.

The story of Enron is a cautionary tale, a dark chapter in the history of corporate America. It serves as a stark reminder of the dangers of a lack of openness and the devastating consequences it can have on employees, investors, and the entire financial system.

While great leaders are celebrated for their decisive decision-making and their ability to envision a future that benefits their organisation, what leaders can do is ensure transparency in their decision-making process, taking feedback and analysing experiences. How does open-mindedness play a role in this crucial process?

Imagine a room filled with talented individuals, each with a unique perspective. What if a few bold voices challenged the status quo? What if there was a space for open dialogue where traditional beliefs were revisited and innovative ideas explored?

No one can predict the future with absolute certainty. A decision that seems brilliant today might not have succeeded without a dissenting voice. Think about our own life. Haven't there been times when we were determined to follow a particular course of action, only to regret it later? Perhaps someone, even with a seemingly "crazy" idea, warned us against it. Now, we wonder, ***"What if I had listened?"***

The power of openness lies in its ability to combat hindsight bias and illuminate blind spots. Remember, in life, we may not always get a second opportunity. Hindsight bias, often called the "knew it all along" effect, is a cognitive bias where events seem more predictable after they have occurred. This leads individuals to believe they would have predicted the outcome more accurately than they actually did, overestimating their predictive abilities.

If an individual falls into the trap of hindsight bias, the decisions they make may not be based on actual facts. This phenomenon is evident in various areas of life. For instance, after significant historical events like the fall of the Berlin Wall or major election results, people often claim they saw it coming, despite widespread uncertainty beforehand. Similarly, a sports fan might believe they knew the outcome of a game all along after their team wins or loses, even though the result was unpredictable.

Hindsight bias can distort our understanding of past events and lead to overconfidence in our predictive abilities. It creates a false sense of inevitability, making it seem like the outcome was obvious from the start. To counteract this bias, open-mindedness is crucial. Open-mindedness involves being receptive to new information, considering alternative viewpoints, and being willing to revise one's beliefs based on new evidence.

Research supports the idea that open-mindedness can help overcome hindsight bias. By actively seeking out diverse perspectives and questioning our assumptions, we can develop a more accurate and nuanced understanding of past events. This approach not only improves decision-making, but also fosters a culture of continuous learning and adaptability.

A study by Arkes et al. in 1988[31, 32, 33] found that encouraging individuals to think about alternative outcomes reduced hindsight bias. This finding aligns with the open-minded approach of considering different possibilities, not just the one that actually occurred. By imagining various scenarios, individuals can better understand that outcomes are not always predictable, and that multiple paths could have been taken.

Similarly, research by Roese and Vohs in 2012 highlighted that promoting a growth mindset, which is closely related to open-mindedness, helps individuals better understand and mitigate hindsight bias.

A growth mindset encourages continuous learning and adaptability, recognising that abilities and understanding can develop over time. This mindset helps individuals remain flexible and open to new information, reducing the tendency to believe that they "knew it all along."

Incorporating open-mindedness into one's cognitive toolkit can significantly reduce hindsight bias. By encouraging diverse perspectives and fostering a culture of open dialogue, leaders can make better-informed decisions.

This approach not only enhances organisational success, but also contributes to personal happiness. Open-mindedness allows for a more accurate assessment of past events and prepares individuals and organisations to navigate future challenges with greater insight and adaptability.

Ultimately, embracing open-mindedness leads to a more nuanced and effective decision-making process, benefiting both professional and personal life.

There is no doubt that by valuing diverse perspectives, we tap into a wellspring of creativity and insight. New ideas spark innovation, pushing the team and business beyond self-imposed limitations. Imagine the power of unleashing a "creative workforce," where individuals feel empowered to share their unique perspectives.

This inclusivity fosters a sense of ownership and fuels engagement, leading to groundbreaking solutions that benefit both individuals and the organisation as a whole.

Openness, a Balance of "Self-belief" and "Receptiveness,"

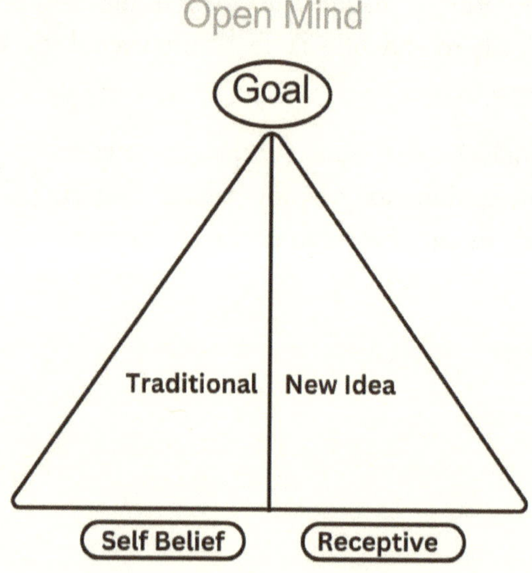

While we have touched upon the significance of openness, it is crucial to strike a balance between self-belief and receptiveness to new ideas.

Openness involves not only confidence in one's abilities and judgements, but also a willingness to consider alternative perspectives and adapt based on new information.

Maintaining this balance is essential for practical goal achievement. Too much self-belief, without receptiveness, can lead to stubbornness and a refusal to acknowledge valuable insights from others. Conversely, being overly receptive, without sufficient self-belief, can result in indecision and a lack of direction. The key is to integrate these two aspects, fostering a mindset that is both confident and flexible.

The graph highlights practical strategies for achieving desired goals through this balanced approach. By combining self-belief with receptiveness, individuals and organisations can navigate challenges more effectively, make well-rounded decisions, and remain open to growth and innovation.

When the objective is to attain a desired goal, balancing traditional beliefs with openness to new ideas plays a crucial role. As individuals, we must find harmony between our self-belief and our receptiveness to alternative perspectives. This balance is essential for identifying the most attainable path to achieving our goals.

Traditional beliefs provide a foundation of stability and confidence, rooted in past experiences and proven strategies. However, an openness to new ideas allows us to adapt and innovate, ensuring we remain flexible and responsive to changing circumstances. By integrating these two aspects, we can navigate obstacles more effectively and make informed decisions.

Self-belief fuels our determination and perseverance, enabling us to stay focused and motivated. On the other hand, receptiveness ensures we are open to learning and growth, considering different viewpoints, and adjusting our approach when necessary. Together, these qualities create a dynamic equilibrium that guides us towards success.

Balancing Self-Belief with Openness

Imagine a mountain we wish to climb. Our traditional beliefs – our knowledge, experience, and core values – represent the sturdy boots on our feet, providing traction and stability on our ascent. However, the terrain might be unfamiliar, and a map, compass, or even a helpful guide (representing openness to new ideas) could prove invaluable in navigating the path most efficiently.

The key lies in striking a balance. This concept can be visualised as a triangle, where the peak represents our goal, and the two supporting points represent: **Self-Belief, (Traditional Beliefs), and Receptiveness (openness to New Ideas)**.

Self-Belief (Traditional Beliefs) encompasses our existing knowledge, experience, and core values. A strong foundation in these beliefs provides the confidence and direction needed to persevere on our journey. Whereas **Receptiveness (Openness to New Ideas)** embodies our willingness to consider different perspectives, approaches, and information. Open-mindedness allows us to adapt to changing circumstances and discover more efficient or innovative routes to our goal.

The ideal balance between these two forces depends entirely on the specific mountain we are trying to climb. Is it a well-worn path, clearly marked, and familiar?

In this case, we can rely more heavily on our own experience and knowledge. *But what if we are venturing into uncharted territory?*

We can rely on our past experiences, drawing from the wisdom we have accumulated over time. However, we must recognise that every journey may lead us into uncharted territory, demanding new strategies and fresh perspectives.

As we embark on this voyage, it is essential to balance our confidence with curiosity, ensuring we remain open to growth and innovation. Together, let us navigate these waters with determination and insight, transforming challenges into opportunities, and setting sail towards a horizon of unparalleled success.

Our past experiences are like sunken treasures, holding the wisdom we have accumulated over time. This invaluable knowledge serves as the ballast that keeps us steady on our voyage. However, every journey may lead us into uncharted waters, demanding fresh perspectives and new strategies. As we embark on this adventure, it is essential to strike a balance between the seasoned sailor's confidence and the wide-eyed explorer's curiosity. We must remain open to growth and innovation, for the most valuable discoveries often lie beyond familiar shores.

Defining Our Course: Every great voyage begins with a destination. In the vast ocean of our professional lives, our guiding star is formed by clearly defined goals. Before diving headfirst into the daily grind, we need to map out our objectives. These goals provide direction and purpose, ensuring we do not get lost in a sea of unprioritised tasks. By striking a balance between unwavering self-belief in our abilities and a thirst for knowledge about the ever-changing landscape, we stay focused on what truly matters: achieving remarkable results in the face of countless possibilities.

Preparation Breeds Success: No captain dives headfirst into the unknown. Before tackling a new project, we need to chart the uncharted waters. This means taking stock of our resources—the skills and experience within the team. We identify established routes, best practices, and lessons learned from past successes. But we do not shy away from uncharted territory, where innovative ideas and groundbreaking solutions may be discovered. By understanding the lay of the professional landscape, we can leverage our experience while simultaneously embracing valuable fresh perspectives. This thorough preparation equips us to make informed decisions, anticipate potential challenges, and navigate the journey with confidence.

A Symphony of Perspectives: A lone sailor rarely conquers the open seas, and the same is true in the workplace. It is time to assemble a diverse crew. We step outside our comfort zones and seek individuals with diverse backgrounds and experiences. By engaging with varied perspectives, we gain a well-rounded understanding of the tasks at hand.

From lively discussions with seasoned colleagues to consulting with external experts, we broaden our approach and gather invaluable insights from every corner of the professional world. Remember, a symphony is more beautiful for its diverse instruments; so, too, is a team for its varied skillsets and fresh ideas.

Embracing Innovation with a Steady Hand: The workplace, like the sea, is full of currents—both familiar and unforeseen. Traditional approaches have their value, but innovation is the wind in our sails, propelling us forward.

We must weigh the pros and cons of both, avoiding the tendency to cling stubbornly to outdated methods or blindly following every passing fad.

A balanced evaluation ensures we make decisions that are both groundbreaking and grounded in reality. By embracing innovation, while still considering the wisdom of past experiences, we become masterful navigators of the ever-changing currents of the professional landscape.

Adaptability is the Rudder: As we gather information and embark on our projects, we must be prepared to adjust our course. The path to our goal might not always be a straight line. Flexibility acts as the rudder that steers us through unexpected challenges, allowing us to seize new opportunities and overcome obstacles. This adaptability helps us navigate unexpected storms and stay on track toward achieving our objectives.

By following these principles, we can become masterful navigators of our own success in the workplace. Remember, the journey itself is just as important as the destination we seek. So, let us unfurl our sails, embrace the unknown, and chart a course that leads us towards a horizon of unparalleled success—together!

Ever wonder why openness is so important?

The answer lies in its connection between individual behaviour and organisational culture. When groups of individuals come together, their interactions naturally influence each other's behaviour. Furthermore, the rules and expectations set by organisations (the "rule set") play a significant role in shaping the overall environment.

This is why it is crucial to understand the power of openness at the individual level. By fostering an attitude of openness within each member, they contribute to a more open and collaborative organisational culture.

In our chapter "The Myth of Hierarchy," we discussed the flow of creativity and the resistance that a noble thought must overcome. As an organisation and its leaders work towards a culture that embraces the transparent and open flow of ideas, it is essential to note that opacity in relationships can sow seeds of distrust and demotivation. When information is hidden, it is natural to feel that either the individual in question is not trustworthy or that the person is not capable of handling such information.

The feelings triggered by a lack of transparency, inconsistencies in information, or a sense that something is not fully disclosed can lead to epistemic suspicion, which is a double-edged sword in corporations.

Studies suggest that epistemic suspicion can hinder trust and productivity, yet it may also sometimes spark innovation. You read that correctly—some studies reflect that a moderate level of epistemic suspicion can actually fuel creative thinking.

A key piece of research by Van Quaquebeke and Paulus (2010), published in the Academy of Management Journal, observed that teams with a moderate level of epistemic suspicion displayed greater creativity than teams with either low or high levels of suspicion. This suggests that moderate suspicion encourages the questioning of assumptions and openness to added information, ultimately leading to a more creative approach to problem-solving.

Research by Paulus and Dzindolet, published in "Organisational Behaviour and Human Decision Processes," examined the role of uncertainty in idea generation. Their findings suggest that moderate levels of uncertainty, similar to epistemic suspicion, can stimulate creative thinking.

Similarly, Nemeth et al. (2001) explored the benefits of "divergent thinking" in creative problem-solving, mentioning that epistemic suspicion can promote this kind of thinking by encouraging individuals to consider alternative perspectives.

Notably, all these studies emphasise the importance of moderation. While social behaviour often associates moderation with irrationality, individual perceptions vary. These findings support the idea that a moderate level of epistemic suspicion can enhance innovation.

However, it is also important to remember that the studies suggest an inverted U-shaped relationship between epistemic suspicion and creativity. Too little suspicion can lead to a lack of critical thinking and an acceptance of the status quo. Conversely, excessive suspicion can create a climate of fear and distrust that stifles creativity.

Numerous studies examine the potential challenges and impacts of epistemic suspicion in the workplace. One notable study published in the Journal of Business Ethics[38] reveals that when employees suspect hidden agendas or perceive a lack of transparency from their leaders, their engagement and productivity significantly diminish. This erosion of trust can lead to a noticeable decline in morale, ultimately dragging down overall performance and fostering a negative work environment.

Adding to this, another research published[39] in Organisation Science highlights how suspicion of manipulation or concealed motives can further complicate workplace dynamics. When employees doubt the integrity of official communications or data, their ability to trust these sources diminishes. This distrust hampers their decision-making processes, often resulting in poor strategic choices and inefficiencies.

These studies underscore the delicate balance required in maintaining a healthy level of transparency and trust within organisations.

They illustrate how easily suspicion can undermine employee engagement and productivity, highlighting the importance of open and honest communication in fostering a positive, and effective work environment.

Excessive suspicion can lead to a state of paralysis by analysis. Employees may become so focused on questioning everything that they become bogged down in overthinking and struggle to take any decisive action. A pervasive climate of suspicion can make it difficult for employees to trust and collaborate with one another. People may be hesitant to share ideas or information for fear of being ridiculed or ostracised. This can hinder teamwork and innovation.

When suspicion runs high, minor disagreements can escalate into major conflicts. Employees may become defensive and unwilling to listen to opposing viewpoints, creating a toxic work environment that makes it difficult to achieve common goals.

While epistemic suspicion can have some positive effects, it is always the organisations that foster open communication, transparency, and trust that can create an environment where healthy questioning can lead to innovation without the negative consequences of excessive suspicion.

Throughout this journey, we have explored the transformative power of openness – its ability to unlock creativity, drive progress, and empower both individuals and organisations.

But remember, openness flourishes only when nurtured by trust and transparency. Like a delicate flower in a sunlit garden, its growth is stunted in the absence of these vital elements.

While individuals shape their professional paths, the fertile ground for openness is cultivated by organisations and their leaders. It is they who have the power to harness the potential of openness, fostering an environment where collaboration thrives, and innovation flourishes.

What Ego Whispers

Let us pause a moment and listen to ego.

Oh, the grandeur! I am the illustrious leader, the beacon of brilliance! Who dares to question the sanctity of my ideas? Absolutely no one, for I simply cannot fathom anyone surpassing my genius. Ah, behold the almighty gatekeeper of right and wrong!

A meeting, you say? Oh, it is merely a congregation where the hallowed seal of approval is bestowed upon what aligns with my divine decree. Fear not, for I possess the unparalleled skill to salvage any sinking ship, all thanks to the incompetence of those who dare not heed my wisdom.

Yes, yes, rest assured, my decisions are as solid as the mountains, fortified by aeons of experience. Bow before the magnificence! Every step I take is a masterstroke, a testament to my unmatched prowess. Those below me, take heed: my words are your gospel; my actions, your blueprint.

In the grand tapestry of success, I am the golden thread, weaving brilliance into every project. So, let us march forth, guided by my vision, towards a future as bright as my brilliance. Remember, in the realm of greatness, there is only one sovereign: me. Now, bask in the glory of my leadership!

Chapter 3

Integrity in Action

In previous chapters, we discussed the importance of clear communication and fostering a culture of open dialogue. But what happens when those words do not translate into action? Imagine a company that boasts a "people-first" philosophy, yet employees consistently face burnout due to unrealistic workloads. Or a leader who champions innovation but shuts down any idea that challenges the status quo. This disconnects between what is said and what has done creates a major dilemma: the "credibility gap."

Think about the most effective teams you have been a part of. Didn't they all share a common thread – a foundation of trust? Leaders who "Walk the Talk," whose actions consistently mirror their words, build this critical bridge. They foster an environment where employees feel respected, valued, and heard. This, in turn, fuels a positive *"conformity,"* where individuals naturally align with the organisation's goals, empowered to contribute their best efforts and collaborate effectively.

This chapter explores the importance of "Walking the Talk" and provides strategies for bridging the "credibility gap" between words and actions. By aligning the leadership style with values, an individual can foster a thriving and trustworthy work environment.

Imagine walking into our trusted bank, known for its friendly service and commitment to our financial well-being. Now, imagine in the same bank, a bank employee, under immense pressure, secretly opens credit cards and bank accounts in our name – all without our knowledge. Shocking, right? That is exactly what happened at Wells Fargo in a scandal[14].

For years, employees were pushed to meet unrealistic sales quotas. Instead of empowering them with the tools to genuinely serve customers, management prioritised numbers at all costs.

The pressure became so intense that employees resorted to creating millions of unauthorised accounts, a blatant violation of trust. This was not just a numbers game; it had real consequences. Customers were left confused, angry, and financially vulnerable. Employees felt conflicted, pressured to meet impossible goals while knowing they were breaking the bank's core principles. The scandal exposed the hollowness of Wells Fargo's "customer-first" slogan, and the actions contradict words.

Wells Fargo's reputation took a nosedive. The bank faced billions in fines, and the senior executives went through tough times. But most importantly, this is one of such corporate stories that serves as a stark reminder: when leaders fail to "Walk the Talk," the consequences can be devastating.

These stories illustrate why "Walking the Talk" is critical. Leaders who consistently translate their words into action foster trust, motivation, and a positive work environment. When actions contradict words, trust erodes, and the consequences can be severe. Remember, a leader's credibility is their most valuable asset, and it is built one action at a time.

Take the Wells Fargo scandal, for example. Were top executives truly oblivious to the deceptive practices festering at lower levels? Of course, the spotlight falls on leadership when employee actions involve manipulating numbers, a blatant betrayal of the company's core values.

When a leadership team proudly proclaims a customer-centric mission, yet the reality paints a starkly different picture, it exposes a critical flaw: a complete lack of mechanisms to safeguard the very principles they preach.

Here is the crux of the matter: Leaders who "Walk the Talk" bridge the gap between words and actions. This translates to building robust systems that not only ensure desired behaviours are implemented, but also provide ongoing evaluation mechanisms. These systems are the guardians of a company's integrity, holding both leaders and employees accountable, while ensuring the path towards achieving objectives remains ethical and transparent.

We naturally judge individuals, institutions, and groups based on their past actions. When actions contradict words or promises, it creates disbelief and undermines *"conformity"* – the idea that people will align with the organisation's goals.

So, for organisations that prioritise integrity and want to build a fortress of trust, sugary pronouncements and empty, unattainable promises simply will not cut it. Leaders must speak in clear, actionable terms. Every word uttered and every action taken matters. They paint a picture of the organisation's true values, and stakeholders will instinctively gauge if this picture aligns with reality.

And so, the next question arises: *if words have such a powerful influence over actions, why is "Walking the Talk" so challenging?*

Why is It so Hard to Walk the Talk?

There is not a single, definitive answer to this question. The difficulty in aligning words with actions can stem from a complex interplay of factors.

Fear, carelessness, situational pressures, and a lack of prioritisation all play their parts. Moreover, the subjective nature of human perception means that people often interpret statements in ways that suit their own interests. This is evident in many areas of life; for instance, in a courtroom, two parties can present drastically different interpretations of the same event, each passionately believing in the validity of their own version of the story.

Culture and its underlying values are built on moral principles, forming a framework that ideally should guide behaviour. For an individual or group to truly "walk the talk," there must be a clear and shared understanding of objectives and vision, coupled with a genuine commitment to achieving those goals.

Each word spoken must be backed by consistent and deliberate actions. Only through this alignment can the integrity of one's words be maintained, ensuring that promises and principles are not just empty rhetoric, but a true reflection of lived reality.

Among the many other roadblocks, sometimes, it is the *fear of failure* that trips an individual the most. They worry about not meeting expectations, losing face, or jeopardising short-term gains. It can be tempting to take a shortcut, to prioritise immediate results over building long-term trust.

For example, imagine a CEO facing pressure from investors to deliver quarterly profits. They might be tempted to cut corners on safety measures or prioritise sales over customer satisfaction. While this approach might boost short-term results, it can ultimately lead to disaster, as we saw in the case of the *'Rana Plaza garment factory' collapse*[40] in Bangladesh, which stands as a tragic testament to this truth. The relentless pursuit of short-term gains at the expense of safety ultimately resulted in a horrifying loss of life. This is a stark reminder for leaders – prioritising "Walking the Talk" might feel challenging in the face of immediate pressures.

This behaviour can be fuelled by two common psychological traps: the ***Loss Aversion*** and the ***Social Desirability Bias***.

Loss Aversion is where an individual tends to weigh potential losses more heavily than equivalent gains. A leader facing a difficult decision might be reluctant to disclose an uncomfortable truth if they fear losing their job or the trust of their board, and the **Social Desirability Bias** is where an individual wants to present themselves favourably. Leaders might withhold information, fearing they will be judged negatively for admitting mistakes or taking risks.

An individual caught in these traps often overlooks potential long-term damage, focusing instead on short-term benefits. This intense focus creates a tunnel vision effect, diverting their attention from the underlying issues simmering beneath the surface. These underlying issues, while not screaming for attention now, could snowball into major problems down the road.

The prioritisation becomes clear – it is all about addressing the most pressing concerns first, the ones demanding immediate attention. Long-term issues, seemingly unaffected by the current frenzy, get pushed to the back burner. This approach, while seemingly practical in the short-term, is akin to neglecting cracks in a dam – a recipe for future disaster.

So, How to Walk the Talk?

Organisations can cultivate a culture of 'walk the talk.' It all starts from top to bottom. Do you remember the quote from the previous chapter, 'The Power of Openness' – ***"Yadha Raja Thadha Prajah,"*** which translates to "As is the king, so are his people"?

Imagine a leader who preaches punctuality to their employees, yet consistently waltzes into meetings late. Or another who enforces rigid policies on everyone, except themselves, conveniently carving out exceptions when the rules apply to them. These scenarios reek of hypocrisy – a leadership style that poisons a company's culture.

When leaders fail to "Walk the Talk," it sends a clear message: their words hold little value. Their actions become the true north star, and employees follow suit. Why arrive on time for a meeting if the leader themself isn't there? Why follow company policies when the leader themselves enjoys a special set of rules?

This phenomenon is rooted in our natural tendency to mimic the behaviours of those around us. We observe, we adapt, and, in this case, we can become part of the problem. It's like social conformity on steroids. We crave acceptance within our group, and if the group norm is to "talk the talk but not walk the walk," we might unconsciously conform to avoid exclusion.

We all like to think our choices are rational and objective. But the truth is, our decisions are often influenced by unconscious biases – mental shortcuts that can lead us astray.

Overcoming decision-making and desirability biases requires a combination of individual and collective efforts.

By understanding and implementing these strategies and fostering an environment of openness and support, both individuals and groups can make more informed, unbiased decisions. This infographic offers a roadmap to tackle these biases, empowering you to make better choices, both individually and collaboratively.

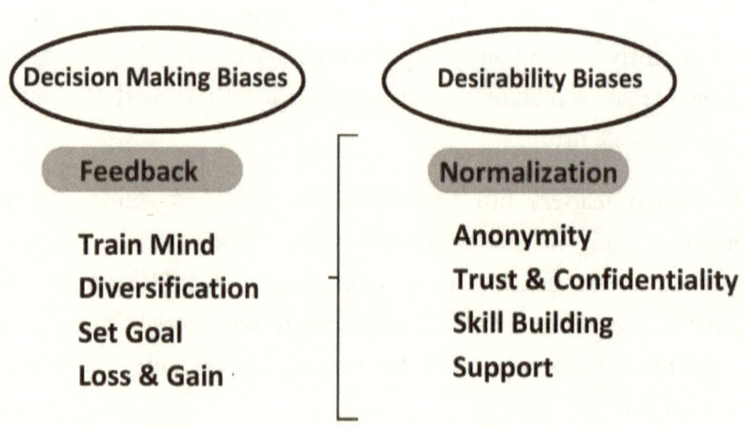

Imagine ourselves navigating a labyrinthine office, where every corner holds hidden challenges, and whispers of bias echo down the twisting corridors. This may feel like our daily reality, but just as a seasoned explorer uses a map to overcome obstacles, we too can equip ourselves with powerful tools to make clear-headed decisions. Let us embark on a journey of self-discovery, a survival guide for navigating the complexities of the modern workplace.

Turning Critique into Golden Opportunities: Picture our colleagues and mentors as wise blacksmiths, holding a fiery torch to our work. Their feedback, like the clanging of hammers on hot metal, may seem harsh at first. But this "criticism" is actually the key to unlocking our full potential. By fostering a culture where feedback is seen as a tool for improvement, not a weapon of negativity, we can transform our workplace experience. Actively seek out constructive criticism, for it refines our thinking and allows us to craft stronger decisions. When a peer points out a potential flaw in our project, view it as an opportunity to forge something even more remarkable.

Facing our Cognitive Dragons: Knowledge is a powerful weapon in the fight against bias. Imagine a monstrous hydra with multiple heads, each representing a different cognitive bias.

One head whisper's, "anchoring bias," urging us to overvalue the first piece of information we receive. Another hisses "loss aversion," filling us with fear of missing out on the familiar, even when presented with exciting new possibilities. By becoming familiar with these biases, we can gain the power to slay them before they can influence our decisions.

Escaping the Echo Chamber: Have you ever been part of a team where everyone agrees with the leader, not out of conviction, but simply to avoid conflict? This is the insidious echo chamber – a breeding ground for uninformed decisions.

Instead, seek out diverse voices and information that challenge your assumptions. Brainstorm with teams that bring a kaleidoscope of perspectives or consult with industry experts who can offer fresh insights. Remember, the richer the tapestry of viewpoints woven into our decision-making process, the more informed and well-rounded your choices will be.

Charting our Course to Success: Clear goals in the workplace are like a beacon in the fog, guiding us towards success. They keep us on the track and prevent us from getting lost in a sea of distractions. However, beware of the siren song of "loss aversion."

Do not let the fear of missing out on past successes blind us to the potential rewards of innovation and growth. Keep our professional goals firmly in sight and let them be our guiding star as we navigate the ever-changing landscape of your career.

Embracing Healthy Disagreements: In team settings, there is a risk of succumbing to "desirability bias," where everyone flocks towards the most popular option, regardless of its effectiveness. Leaders must be champions of open discourse, fostering environments where diverse opinions are not just tolerated but actively encouraged.

Imagine a leader as a skilled shepherd, gently guiding the team through challenging terrain. They ensure every voice is heard, allowing the team to navigate towards the most successful outcome.

Creating Safe Spaces for Honest Feedback: Sometimes, employees hesitate to share their true thoughts for fear of judgement. Leaders can counteract this by creating safe spaces for open discussion. Normalise the expression of diverse opinions and implement anonymous feedback mechanisms.

This is like building a magical suggestion box where everyone can contribute their honest insights without fear. By fostering a culture of psychological safety, where vulnerability is seen as strength, you can unlock a treasure trove of valuable perspectives.

Building Bridges through Dialogue: Effective communication is the golden thread that binds successful teams together. Imagine a team as a magnificent tapestry, where diverse perspectives are woven into a cohesive whole. By honing communication skills, assertiveness, and conflict resolution techniques, teams can navigate disagreements constructively. Healthy debate is not a battlefield, but a crucible where the most well-rounded and informed decisions are forged.

Ultimately, overcoming decision-making bias boils down to fostering a culture of psychological safety. This means creating an environment where individuals feel comfortable expressing their true thoughts without fear of reprisal. By embracing open communication, diverse perspectives, and continuous learning, both individuals and groups can make smarter, more effective decisions. Picture a workplace where honesty becomes second nature, not an obligation.

Leaders play a crucial role in this quest. Great leaders are courageous, making decisions and learning from both successes and failures.

This willingness to be vulnerable and embrace the unknown separates good leaders from genuinely great ones. It is like a captain navigating the troop to the unknown and guiding them to success.

Imagine yourself on a battlefield, the adrenaline pumping through your veins. Your trusted commander barks orders, directing your team towards the enemy position. You grab your weapon, fuelled by the unwavering belief in your leader's strategy. This trust is not blind faith; it is the result of consistent, decisive leadership that inspires confidence.

Now, picture a different scenario. The same battlefield, but the orders are confusing and constantly changing. March forward. No, wait, come back! The once-clear direction dissolves into a chaotic mess. Fear might keep us silent initially, but trust crumbles with each contradictory command. How long can we follow a leader who seems as lost?

This battlefield analogy illustrates the critical role of trust in leadership. Whether a CEO navigating a competitive market or a president leading a nation, trust is the invisible thread that binds followers to their leader. People are willing to follow when they believe their leader walks the talk – that actions align with words, and decisions are made with an unobstructed vision. A confused and unconfident leader cannot control its followers.

Inconsistent leadership erodes trust at an alarming rate. When a leader's actions contradict their pronouncements, confusion and doubt take root. Just like the bewildered soldier on the battlefield, followers lose confidence in their leader's ability to guide them through challenges. This lack of trust leads to a breakdown in communication, disengagement, and, ultimately, a failure to achieve goals.

Great leaders understand that consistency is key. They make well-considered decisions, communicate them clearly, and then follow through with resolute action.

Even when faced with unexpected situations, they demonstrate the flexibility to adapt without compromising their core values. This unwavering commitment builds a foundation of trust, empowering followers to move forward with confidence, even in the face of uncertainty.

Trust is a fragile thing, easily shattered by inconsistency. Leaders who consistently "Walk the Talk" are the ones who inspire loyalty, foster collaboration, and, ultimately, lead their followers to victory – whether on a physical battlefield or in the complex landscapes of business and society.

This revised version uses vivid imagery and a relatable story to highlight the importance of consistent leadership. It emphasises the consequences of indecisiveness and the power of trust in achieving success.

What Ego Whispers

Let's pause a moment and listen to ego.

Some things are hush-hush for a reason, you know? Spilling the beans could sink the ship! But hey, I'm the captain of success here. Risky business? No sweat, I'm all about that high-risk, high-reward life. I'm not just all talk, you know.

Sure, I might change my mind last minute, but hey, that's just how the cookie crumbles! Flexibility is key in this game, and I wield it like a sword. Decisions, after all, need that touch of brilliance, only I can provide.

When it comes to steering this ship, I navigate through storms with a confident grin. Sure, some might call it reckless, but I call it visionary. While others fret about the details, I keep my eye on the prize, making bold moves that keep us afloat and thriving.

So, to all the naysayers and doubters, remember this: I'm the one turning risks into rewards, making magic happen from chaos. Sit back, relax, and watch as I masterfully steer us to glory, one unpredictable turn at a time. After all, who doesn't love a bit of excitement in their success story?

Chapter 4

Fair Rewards and Earned Recognition

Imagine a vibrant workplace – a place where employees feel valued, motivated, and inspired to excel. We've already discussed the importance of building a strong foundation: an open culture, fuelled by transparency and integrity.

But, how do we take it further? How do we create an environment that doesn't just function, but truly thrives?

The solution is multifaceted, yet one undeniable factor that must be considered is the strategic implementation of rewards and recognition. However, there is a surprising twist: many organisations offer reward programmes they believe are adequate, yet employees often feel undervalued.

Think about it – have you ever received a generic award that felt more like a box to check than a genuine recognition of your efforts? This disconnect between perception and reality can be a real morale killer, leading to decreased productivity and a sense of disengagement.

The problem isn't the absence of rewards; it's their misalignment with what truly motivates employees. Picture this – a company showers its top sellers with bonuses. While a nice gesture, it might not resonate with everyone. What about those who value meaningful feedback or opportunities to grow their skills? A one-size-fits-all approach leaves many feeling undervalued.

Here's the secret weapon the organisation can make use of: 'appreciation.' It's a fundamental human need, and when employees feel recognised for their contributions, it fuels a powerful engine of motivation, engagement, and loyalty. Studies show that appreciated employees go the extra mile, innovate with passion, and become champions for their organisations. Strategic reward and recognition programmes can bridge the gap between how employers perceive their efforts and how employees feel valued.

Let's illustrate this through a story. Imagine *John*, a dedicated employee who consistently excels for years. He's a master multitasker, highly respected by colleagues, and regularly receives top performance ratings. Now, picture *Peter*, another top performer responsible for key operations. However, Peter enjoys a higher benefits package.

While John is genuinely happy for Peter's success, a question arises in his mind: ***"Why am I not being considered? Are my contributions less valuable?"*** John's smile vanished, replaced by a frown of confusion and simmering resentment. Why?

This scenario is all too common. Many employees feel undervalued when they see new hires entering the company at higher salaries for the same role they've been fulfilling for years.

John's reaction isn't some personal quirk; it's a classic case of psychological and organisational theories at play.

We all have an innate sense of fairness. When we perceive a situation as unequal – such as putting in the same effort but receiving fewer rewards – it throws us off balance. John might feel undervalued, questioning why his dedication seems less appreciated than Peter's.

To understand John's reaction, we must first step into his shoes. By examining the psychological underpinnings of his response, we can gain valuable insights into his motivations and perspectives.

A fundamental question arises: **Whose fault is it?** This query serves as a starting point for unravelling the complex web of emotions and perceptions at play.

- **The Comparison Trap:** John might be playing a dangerous game called *'social comparison'*. We often gauge ourselves against others. In this case, John compares his benefits package to Peter's, and the result stings. This unfavourable comparison can breed frustration and even envy. John might think, "We both perform exceptionally, yet Peter gets the better deal?" It's a recipe for a dip in morale.

- **The Motivation Maze:** John likely expected his stellar performance to be met with a competitive benefits package. The reality shatters his expectations. Expectancy theory explains this. We're motivated by anticipated outcomes. If John believed exceptional work meant top-tier benefits, the realisation that this isn't the case can be disillusioning. The disconnect between effort and reward can seriously dent his motivation. *Why put in the extra effort if the payoff isn't there?*

- **The Blame Game:** John might be asking, *"Why me?"* Attribution theory examines how we assign blame. If John perceives the benefits gap as unjustified, perhaps due to favouritism or unfair policies, he might feel powerless and out of control. This perception can lead to demotivation and a sense of resignation. John might think, "What's the point if my efforts don't matter?"

These highlight the importance of **organisational justice**[20], the perception of fairness in the workplace. When employees, like John, feel unfairly treated, it erodes trust, commitment, and, ultimately, productivity.

When employees perceive inequity in the distribution of rewards or resources, it can undermine their trust in the organisation and reduce their commitment and engagement. John's reaction to the perceived unfairness in benefits allocation reflects his assessment of organisational justice within the company.

John's case isn't unique. Many organisations struggle with hidden biases and a lack of transparency, leading to a feeling of inequity among employees.

So, why do these disparities persist, leaving employees like John feeling undervalued? Let us peek behind some of the scenes and explore the potential culprits.

- **Inequitable Compensation Practices**: Imagine a tangled web of policies and procedures. This web could be the culprit behind John's situation. Inequitable compensation practices can create unintended gaps in benefits packages, even for employees with similar performance. Inconsistent evaluation methods, subjective decisions by managers, or a lack of transparency, in how rewards are allocated, can all contribute to this labyrinth.

- **Managerial Bias**: John might be a victim of unconscious bias. Managers, despite their best intentions, can favour certain employees. This managerial bias can lead to unequal distribution of rewards, creating a perception of unfairness and eroding trust in leadership. John might wonder, "Why is Peter getting a better deal when we both perform well?"

- **The Blind Spot**: Sometimes, knowledge is the missing piece. HR departments or senior leadership might be unaware of these disparities. Competing priorities or limited resources can make it difficult to see the bigger picture. Without systems to monitor and address compensation gaps, they can linger unnoticed. John might think, "No one seems to care that I'm getting the short end of the stick."

- **The Broken Culture**: Every organisation has a personality. If fairness and equity are not core values, John might feel like his voice would not be heard. An organisational culture that prioritises connections over fairness can breed a sense of powerlessness in employees. John might think, "What's the point of speaking up if nothing will change?"

- **Communication Barriers:** Fear can be a powerful silencer. John might hesitate to speak up about the disparity due to fear of retaliation, a lack of clear channels for feedback, or simply a feeling that his concerns would not be addressed. These communication barriers prevent open dialogue and can leave John feeling unheard.

- **Resource Constraints:** Sometimes, it is a matter of resources. The organisation might be facing budget limitations, competing priorities, or lack the expertise to address compensation disparities effectively. These resource constraints can make it difficult to implement changes, even if they are desired. John might think, "They probably want to fix this, but they just don't have the resources."

- **The Accountability Gap:** Without consequences for unfair practices, what is the incentive to change? A lack of accountability mechanisms can allow compensation disparities to persist. John might think, "If nothing happens when things are unfair, why should I expect it to be different this time?"

The good news is that these issues can be addressed. By aligning compensation with values, fostering transparency, implementing bias training, and building robust systems for monitoring and fixing inequities, organisations can create a more equitable workplace. This will make John and all employees feel valued and fairly rewarded for their contributions.

Addressing these through transparent, fair reward systems and efforts to promote equity and justice in the workplace can help mitigate such negative reactions and maintain employee morale and motivation.

So, how do we design programmes that truly connect with our workforce? The key is a multi-pronged approach:

- **Unveiling Employee Desires:** It all starts with understanding what truly motivates our team. Surveys, focus groups, and open conversations can reveal what forms of recognition hold the most weight – consideration based on generation, position, and individual preferences.

- **More Than Money:** Financial rewards can play a role, but don't underestimate the power of non-monetary recognition. Public praise, personalised feedback, professional development opportunities, or flexible work arrangements can all be powerful motivators.

- **Values Take Centre Stage:** Effective programmes reinforce your organisation's core values. Is teamwork a cornerstone? Consider recognising collaborative achievements.

- **Clarity and Communication:** Transparency is key. Clearly communicate programme details, eligibility criteria, and how recognition is awarded. This eliminates confusion and fosters trust.

- **The Power of "Now":** Appreciation shouldn't be an annual event. Regular recognition, both formal and informal, keeps employees engaged and motivated throughout the year.

By strategically revamping the reward and recognition programmes, organisations can bridge the gap between perceived and actual appreciation. The result could be a more motivated, productive, and positive workforce, ready to unlock its full potential. This isn't just about rewards – it's about creating a workplace where people feel valued, respected, and inspired to do their best work.

To truly understand the complexities of fairness, we must delve into the psychological underpinnings that shape our perceptions. let's keep these three intriguing concepts in mind:

> *The **just-world hypothesis**. It's a way our brains make sense of the world, where we believe good things happen to good people, and vice versa. This can lead us to interpret events in a way that reinforces this belief, even if the reality is more complex.*
>
> *The concept of **conformity**, which describes the tendency of individuals to adjust their thoughts, behaviours, and attitudes to align with group norms, even when these norms are flawed or illogical.*
>
> *The **Cognitive dissonance** which is a psychological phenomenon that occurs when an individual experiences conflicting thoughts, beliefs, or attitudes.*

Now, Let's get back through the story of John. *John* holds a belief that **Ruby**, a coworker, is not a good team player due to past disagreements and clashes.

Despite John's negative perception of Ruby, he notices that Ruby consistently receives promotions, bonuses, and praise from management for her work. Ruby's projects are successful, and she is often recognised as a high performer within the organisation. Meanwhile, John observes another coworker, Rasha, whom he perceives as more agreeable and competent; however, she is facing challenges and setbacks in their projects. Despite Rasha's hard work and dedication, she receives less recognition and advancement opportunities compared to Ruby. John's belief in the *just-world hypothesis* leads him to expect that hard work and competence will be rewarded, while laziness or incompetence will be punished.

This belief shapes his worldview and how he interprets events in the workplace, but when Ruby receives a promotion, it creates psychological disagreement for John.

This state of discomfort or tension, known as *cognitive dissonance*, occurs as the individual seeks to reconcile the conflicting cognitions. To reduce this discomfort, individuals may engage in various reasoning processes, such as rationalisation or justification, to bring their beliefs or behaviours into alignment with one another.

When groups of individuals operate under the principles of '*conformity*' and the '*just-world hypothesis*,' the impact on an organisation can be profound and far-reaching. To navigate this challenge, it is essential to foster a culture of transparency, openness, and integrity. These elements form the cornerstone of a successful work environment.

Consider the findings of a 2021 study published in the Journal of Nursing Administration, which examined data from over 1,800 hospitals. The study found a direct correlation between nurse pay dissatisfaction and increased hospital costs. Hospitals with significant pay discrepancies between nurses and other staff experienced higher turnover rates among nurses and increased spending on temporary staffing agencies.

This evidence underscores the financial implications of unfair reward structures. When compensation is perceived as unjust, it not only affects employee morale, but also leads to tangible financial losses for the organisation. Therefore, addressing these disparities through transparent practices and a commitment to fairness is not just a moral imperative, but a strategic necessity for organisational success.

Adding to this, the 2017 lawsuit by the Department of Labour against Google accused the tech giant of systematically underpaying female employees in tech roles. This high-profile case highlighted the pervasiveness of gender bias in compensation practices, sending shockwaves through the corporate world.

The evidence is irrefutable: studies and real-world examples overwhelmingly point to the critical importance of fair reward and recognition policies. Humans are inherently driven to grow and thrive in environments that offer equitable opportunities. Organisations, and the leaders who guide them, cannot afford to disregard this fundamental human need. Failure to address these disparities can lead to a demoralised workforce, ultimately eroding productivity and success.

Rewards are a powerful motivator, with numerous studies showing that a satisfied employee is a productive one. However, rewards are just one piece of the puzzle. It is the responsibility of leaders and organisations to design a fair reward mechanism that fosters a culture where excellence is truly recognised.

Imagine a stagnant environment where nothing bad happens, but nothing good happens either. This lack of progress contradicts our human nature – we crave growth and recognition. Leaders who think, "Well, at least we weren't bad to them!" are missing the mark. Employees deserve better – better rewards and support to fuel their motivation and ambition.

Think of an organisation as a garden. In a healthy environment, vibrant plants thrive, pushing out weeds. Similarly, a positive culture fosters productive and happy employees. When reward and recognition policies are well-designed, the organisation creates fertile ground for employee growth. Minor setbacks and disappointments become opportunities to learn and improve, just as weeds can't compete with healthy plants.

The key is appropriate rewards. A cookie-cutter approach won't do. Rewards need to be meaningful and personalised to truly motivate individuals. Imagine a leader who recognises an employee's exceptional performance, not just with a generic plaque, but with an opportunity for professional development or a chance to tackle a challenging new project. That's the kind of recognition that fuels engagement and a desire to excel.

By creating a culture that values and rewards excellence fairly, organisations can cultivate a thriving garden of motivated and productive employees. This isn't just about handing out trophies; it's about creating an environment where employees feel valued, empowered, and excited to come to work and do their best work.

What Ego Whispers

Let's pause a moment and listen to ego.

Rewards go to those who earn them, but sometimes exceptions are needed to keep the organisation thriving. Talent is vital, even if it means making some adjustments. I always prioritise what's best for the entire organisation.

When key players are content and recognised, it paves the way for overall success. After all, happy talent equals a happy company. And who's guiding us toward that success? You guessed it, me – the leader who knows how to steer this ship!

I've mastered the delicate balance of rewarding hard work and making strategic exceptions. It's not just about fairness; it's about ensuring we stay at the top. Sure, some may say I play favourites, but in reality, I'm just a connoisseur of talent. I know how to keep our top performers happy and productive.

Think of me as the maestro of motivation, the conductor of commendations. With every decision, I am not just looking at today's success, but tomorrow's triumphs. Keeping the best and brightest satisfied is a surefire way to maintain our edge.

So, when you see our organisation thriving, remember who is behind the wheel. That is right, it is me – the visionary leader who knows how to make the tough calls and steer us toward greatness. Bow before the brilliance!

Chapter 5

Support as Investment

The previous chapters explored the concept of fair rewards and recognition in shaping employee motivation and satisfaction. While we establish that fairness is a cornerstone of a healthy work environment, human beings are driven by more than just tangible rewards. We crave a sense of belonging, purpose, and support.

Imagine a talented employee who consistently delivers exceptional work. They are motivated by recognition and financial rewards, of course, but what truly fosters loyalty and commitment goes beyond a paycheck.

This employee thrives in an environment where they feel supported by their organisation and their leader. This support manifests in numerous ways: access to resources, opportunities for growth, and a sense of belonging in a team environment.

In the previous chapter, we tried to explore the concept of fair rewards and recognition in shaping employee motivation and satisfaction, establishing that fairness is a cornerstone of a healthy work environment. However, if we dig a little deeper, we will discover that human beings crave more than just tangible rewards. We yearn for a sense of belonging, purpose, and a supportive hand to guide us.

Imagine a talented employee who consistently delivers exceptional work. While they are motivated by recognition and financial rewards, what truly fosters their loyalty and commitment goes beyond a paycheck. An employee thrives in an environment where they feel supported by their organisation and leader. This support manifests in numerous ways; it could be access to resources, opportunities for growth, and a sense of belonging in a team environment.

Visualise this: an employee flourishing in a workplace where their efforts are not only acknowledged but also nurtured. They receive the tools and resources needed to excel, are offered pathways for professional development, and feel an integral part of a cohesive team. This sense of belonging and support is what transforms an excellent job into a great one, driving the employee to remain committed and engaged.

By recognising that employees seek more than just financial incentives, organisations can create a more holistic approach to motivation. This involves building a culture where employees feel valued, have a clear sense of purpose, and know they are part of a supportive community. Such an environment not only enhances satisfaction, but also fosters long-term loyalty and dedication.

While we dive deeper into the chapter, let us visit an inspiring tale from Starbucks[24], a company celebrated not just for its exceptional coffee, but also for its groundbreaking approaches to employee benefits and ownership. Among its most remarkable initiatives is the Employee Stock Ownership Programme (ESOP). This programme offers employees the opportunity to become shareholders, turning them into true stakeholders in the company's success. Through ESOP, Starbucks doesn't just serve coffee; it cultivates a sense of ownership and pride among its workforce, fostering a community where every cup poured is a shared achievement.

The origins of Starbucks' Employee Stock Ownership Programme (ESOP) can be traced back to the company's early days when it faced significant financial challenges. At that time, Howard Schultz, the visionary CEO, recognised that the key to the company's success lay in its employees.

In 1991, Schultz introduced the revolutionary Bean Stock programme, granting stock options to all employees, including part-time workers. This bold move was designed to instil a sense of ownership and commitment among Starbucks' workforce, fostering a culture where every employee could share in the company's journey.

The necessity of implementing such a programme stemmed from Schultz's vision of building a company culture centred around shared success. By giving employees a stake in the company's performance, Starbucks aimed to align their interests with those of the shareholders. Furthermore, offering stock ownership became a powerful tool for attracting and retaining talent, providing employees with an opportunity to build wealth alongside the company's growth.

The impact of Starbucks' ESOP has been profound on multiple fronts. Firstly, it has contributed to fostering a strong sense of loyalty and commitment among employees. When individuals have a direct financial stake in the company's success, they are more motivated to perform at their best and contribute to its growth. Secondly, the ESOP has helped create a more inclusive and egalitarian workplace culture. By extending stock ownership to all employees, regardless of their position or level within the company, Starbucks promotes a sense of equality and shared purpose.

Lastly, the ESOP has played a crucial role in driving Starbucks' growth and success. By empowering employees as stakeholders, Starbucks leverages their collective efforts and ideas to enhance customer experiences, and drive innovation. This sense of ownership and involvement translates into higher levels of customer satisfaction and, ultimately, improved financial performance.

Overall, Starbucks' Employee Stock Ownership Programme has transformed the company by fostering a culture of ownership, inclusion, and innovation. It stands as a testament to the power of aligning employee interests with those of the company, ultimately driving long-term success and sustainability.

Let's examine Starbucks' Employee Stock Ownership Plan (ESOP) as a shining example of "Walking the Talk" in action. By offering employees a stake in the company's success, Starbucks aligned their words with their actions, demonstrating a genuine commitment to employee well-being. This powerful move fosters trust and loyalty, two cornerstones of a thriving organisation.

Trust and loyalty aren't handed out; they're earned. The Starbucks ESOP exemplifies this principle. By offering a tangible stake in the company's future, Starbucks sent a clear message: "We value you, and your contributions matter." This kind of genuine investment in employees naturally breeds loyalty and a sense of shared purpose.

Employee recognition and rewards are powerful motivators, but true employee support goes beyond a pat on the back. It's about fostering overall well-being, a multi-faceted concept that encompasses more than just physical health.

Think of well-being as a three-legged stool. One leg represents physical well-being – healthy habits and a strong body. The second leg is financial well-being – feeling secure about your financial future. The third leg is mental well-being – managing stress, maintaining a positive outlook, and feeling emotionally balanced. By supporting all aspects of employee well-being, organisations create a sense of belonging. Employees who feel valued, not just for their work, but for their overall well-being, are more likely to be engaged, productive, and loyal.

Referring to an ancient Sanskrit proverb, *"Karmanye vadhikaraste Ma Phaleshu Kadachana,"* which translates to "Do your duty without the expectation of reward," we find wisdom that may seem at odds with the numbers-driven world of business, where ROI (Return on Investment) is king. However, a deeper understanding reveals its true value. The proverb doesn't advocate ignoring results – achieving employee loyalty remains a critical objective. Instead, it emphasises the importance of sincerity and long-term commitment.

In the realm of business, this ancient wisdom teaches us that while results are important, they should not be the sole focus. It's the dedication to one's duties and the integrity behind actions that build a solid foundation for long-term success. Achieving employee loyalty isn't just about the immediate returns or rewards; it's about fostering a sincere and committed work environment.

By adopting this principle, businesses can cultivate a culture where employees are motivated by more than just immediate rewards. They become driven by a sense of purpose and dedication to their roles, ultimately leading to a more engaged and loyal workforce. This approach, though seemingly counterintuitive in a ROI-centric world, can lead to sustainable success and a more harmonious workplace.

Just like planting a seed requires patience and nurturing, so does the effort to support employee well-being. The fruits of these efforts may not be immediate, but they ultimately yield a loyal and engaged workforce. The story of Starbucks beautifully exemplifies this principle. Their unwavering commitment to employee well-being, even when short-term gains were uncertain, has cultivated a culture of loyalty that drives their long-term success.

Remember our discussion on conformity from previous chapters? The same principles apply to employee support. When individuals feel supported by their organisation and colleagues, a powerful synergy takes root. This sense of belonging and shared purpose creates a ripple effect, inspiring others to reciprocate the support they receive.

Imagine an employee facing a personal crisis – illness, a flooded basement, a car breakdown – reaching out to their "workplace family" for support. They might need a temporary flexible schedule, a short leave of absence, or simply a kind word and a listening ear. But instead of encountering a helping hand, they are met with rigid policies and a bureaucratic maze.

What Would Be the Expected Outcome?

Discouraging, right? That feeling of being abandoned when support is needed most can be incredibly damaging to morale and loyalty.

Now, contrast this with a team where helping hands are readily available. Colleagues step up to meet tight deadlines together, offer guidance through professional challenges, and celebrate both individual and collective wins. This supportive environment fosters not just motivation, but a deeper loyalty – a loyalty that goes beyond a paycheck. By creating such a nurturing atmosphere, organisations can inspire a profound commitment that drives both personal and professional growth.

Why is this loyalty so crucial?

Loyal employees are the bedrock of any thriving organisation. Countless success stories demonstrate the undeniable link between a dedicated team and a company's prosperity. But loyal employees are more than just productive; they become brand ambassadors, enthusiastically advocating for the organisation and its values. They see their well-being intertwined with the company's growth, creating a win-win situation for everyone.

Consider employee support like catching a cold. Preventing it and addressing it early with a dose of TLC (Tender Loving Care) can prevent it from turning into a full-blown productivity and loyalty killer. Similarly, offering timely support when an employee faces challenges demonstrates genuine care and strengthens the bond with the "workplace family."

Some might see bending the rules or offering flexible support as an added cost. But consider this: a happy, supported employee is a loyal, engaged employee. Loyal, engaged employees are more productive, miss fewer days, and even become brand ambassadors for the organisation. Extending support to employees is a strategic, long-term investment.

While supporting employees yields substantial returns, organisations often overlook essential support mechanisms. This neglect isn't born of indifference, but rather a complex interplay of priorities and the elusive nature of immediate gains. Like the other facets we've explored, there is no simple answer to this conundrum. Yet, the concept of prioritisation looms large.

Organisations tend to focus on immediate, tangible achievements. Imagine the exhilaration of watching sales figures climb or revenue graphs soar. These metrics provide clear, observable improvements that are easy to measure and celebrate. The connection between action and result is direct and satisfying – invest in marketing and witness a spike in sales; streamline operations and enjoy increased revenue.

However, investing in employee support is a different story. It's akin to planting a seed and waiting for it to bloom. The benefits are profound but often subtle and slow to manifest. When an organisation allocates resources to employee support, the returns are not immediately visible. There's no instant gratification, no immediate surge in the numbers that stakeholders can point to and say, "Look, our investment paid off!"

Yet, the long-term rewards are invaluable. A workforce that feels genuinely supported and valued will remain loyal and engaged, driving sustained success for the organisation. This investment in people ultimately creates a strong foundation for enduring prosperity, proving that nurturing employee loyalty is as essential as any immediate business metric.

The challenge deepens with the question of efficacy: How can an organisation ensure that its support is reaching those who genuinely need it? Is the support making a meaningful difference, or is it merely a gesture, a line drawn in water that fades without a trace? This uncertainty can make decision-makers hesitant. They fear that the resources dedicated to employee support might dissipate without yielding the desired outcomes, like trying to capture mist in their hands.

Furthermore, the impact of employee support often unfolds quietly and over time. It shows up in reduced turnover, increased job satisfaction, and enhanced productivity, but these indicators don't always make headlines. They are like the roots of a tree, growing strong and deep out of sight, providing the stability and nourishment needed for the organisation to thrive. Yet, the organisations that do invest in their employees, that choose to water these unseen roots, often find themselves rewarded in ways that transcend immediate metrics. They cultivate a loyal, motivated workforce, and this foundation of support becomes their greatest strength. The return on investment in employee support may not be as instant as a spike in sales, but it is just as real and far more enduring.

While we recognise the importance of employee support and its profound relevance, it's equally vital to understand the dynamics of group culture and mindset. When individuals come together in a workplace, the collective mentality shapes the group's culture. This is where psychological concepts like the **_Just-World Hypothesis_** and _conformity_ come into play, influencing perceptions and behaviours in subtle, yet powerful ways.

Consider a scenario where employees perceive that the support mechanisms in place favour a select group of individuals, rather than being equitably distributed.

This perception can be especially damaging. When the belief that good things happen to good people is contradicted by the reality of the workplace, it creates a sense of injustice and dissatisfaction. Employees begin to experience *cognitive dissonance*. On one hand, they want to believe in a fair and just workplace; on the other hand, they see evidence that suggests otherwise.

This dissonance can ripple through the group, undermining morale and cohesion. If employees feel that support mechanisms are biased or ineffective, it can erode trust and loyalty, leading to a more complex and challenging organisational climate.

The sense of injustice can become a breeding ground for discontent, reducing overall productivity and engagement.

Therefore, it is crucial to design and implement support mechanisms that are transparent, fair, and genuinely accessible to all employees.

A system perceived as equitable will foster a positive group culture, reinforcing the belief that good things do indeed happen to those who deserve them. This approach not only addresses the psychological needs of individuals but also strengthens the entire organisation by promoting trust, inclusivity, and a shared sense of purpose.

By ensuring that support is clear and fairly distributed, organisations can mitigate the negative effects of cognitive dissonance and conformity, creating an environment where every employee feels valued and supported. This, in turn, nurtures a culture of fairness and mutual respect, laying the foundation for a more harmonious and productive workplace.

Imagine our organisation as a bustling city. Every employee plays a crucial role, contributing their unique talents and skills. But, just like any city, there will be times when people need a helping hand. Here's where a well-designed support mechanism comes in – a system built not just on logic, but on genuine care for the workforce.

Implementing an effective support mechanism within an organisation is both an art and a science, requiring a delicate balance of fairness, transparency, and genuine care for employees. To truly make a difference, this system must be thoughtfully designed and consistently upheld, ensuring it reaches every individual equitably.

We can approach crafting such a support mechanism step by step:

- **Step 1:** *Assess Needs Thoroughly* - Begin by conducting a comprehensive assessment of your employees' needs through surveys, focus groups, and one-on-one interviews. The goal is to gather diverse perspectives and understand the unique challenges and concerns faced by different members of your workforce. By listening attentively, you can identify the specific areas where support is most needed.

- **Step 2:** *Design with Transparency* - Once you have a clear understanding of the needs, design a support mechanism that is transparent and easily understood by all employees. Transparency builds trust and ensures that everyone knows what support is available, how to access it, and who is eligible. Document the process in clear, straightforward language, and make this information readily accessible.

- **Step 3:** *Ensure Fair Access* - Fairness is the cornerstone of an effective support system. Ensure that the criteria for receiving support are objective and consistently applied. This helps avoid any perception of favouritism or bias. Utilise data-driven approaches to determine eligibility and distribution of resources, making the process as impartial as possible.

- **Step 4:** *Train and Empower Leaders* - Leaders and managers play a pivotal role in the success of support mechanisms. Provide them with training to recognise signs of employee distress and equip them with the tools to offer initial support and guidance. Empower these leaders to act as conduits between the workforce and the support services, fostering a culture of care and responsiveness.

- **Step 5:** *Implement and Communicate* - With the framework in place, launch the support mechanism with a robust communication strategy. Use multiple channels—emails, meetings, intranet, and workshops—to inform employees about the available support. Emphasise the organisation's commitment to their well-being and encourage them to make use of the services without hesitation.

- **Step 6:** *Monitor and Adapt* - An effective support mechanism is not static; it evolves with the needs of the workforce. Regularly monitor the usage and effectiveness of the support services. Collect feedback from employees and analyse the data to identify trends and areas for improvement. Be prepared to adapt and refine the mechanism to ensure it continues to meet the needs of your employees.

- **Step 7:** *Foster a Supportive Culture* - Finally, embed the support mechanism within the broader organisational culture. Promote values of empathy, inclusivity, and mutual support. Recognise and celebrate stories of employees who have benefited from the support system. By integrating these values into the everyday life of the organisation, we can create an environment where support is not just a policy, but a lived experience.

A Living Example

Imagine a company where these steps are meticulously followed. Employees at all levels feel heard and valued. They know exactly where to turn when they need help, and they trust that the support they receive will be fair and effective. Leaders are not just managers, but mentors who guide and support their teams with empathy. This culture of care and support translates into a motivated, engaged workforce that drives the organisation towards its goals with unity and purpose.

In this scenario, the just-world hypothesis aligns more closely with reality: good things do happen to those who contribute positively to the workplace. The support mechanism becomes a testament to the organisation's commitment to its people, reinforcing the belief that every individual matters.

Support, when extended at the right time to deserving individuals, possesses immense power. It can forge long-term loyalty and a deep sense of belonging.

Similarly, if an organisation boasts a "supportive culture" but fails to deliver, the employee experiences a sense of betrayal. Trust crumbles, leading to a decline in morale and, ultimately, a desire to seek employment elsewhere.

Remember the discussion of **cognitive dissonance**? *"Where employees who experience a disconnect between an organisation's stated values and its actual behaviour will inevitably feel frustrated and dissatisfied. This applies to support as well."*

Leaders set the tone for any organisation. Their actions speak volumes. A leader who walks the talk by genuinely supporting their team builds trust, fosters loyalty, and motivates employees beyond the limitations of rewards alone. This intrinsic motivation creates a more engaged and productive workforce, ultimately leading to organisational success. We discussed this in detail in our chapter 'Walk on the Talk.'

An appropriate support mechanism—one rooted in transparency, fairness, and equal treatment—cultivates an unbreakable culture. It fosters leaders who lead by example, a system of rewards and recognition that is clear and just, and a foundation of unwavering support. Such a framework not only sustains the organisation but propels it forward, ensuring its enduring success and vitality in the ever-evolving game of business.

What Ego Whispers

Let's pause a moment and listen to ego.

I'm all for backing up employees, but let's not confuse support with taking advantage. We're here to run a business, not a charity. Rewards are earned through hard work, and support goes to those who truly deserve it. I've got the backs of those who prove their worth – no doubt about it!

While I champion my team, I'm also keen on fairness and merit. This isn't a free-for-all where anyone can ride the coattails of others. No, here, dedication and results speak volumes. If you put in the effort and show your value, you can count on my unwavering support.

Don't get me wrong, I believe in fostering a positive and supportive work environment. But let's be clear: support is for those who earn it through diligence and results. I'm not running a charity, after all. We're all here to achieve greatness, and that requires everyone pulling their weight.

So, to those who work hard and show their worth, rest assured, I've got your back. Together, we'll drive this business to new heights. To everyone else, remember: success is earned, not given. Let's roll up our sleeves and make it happen!

Chapter 6

Penta Factor

As we embark on this exciting new chapter, let's take a moment to reflect on the incredible journey we've shared through the previous ones.

Remember venturing into the labyrinthine world of *"The Dynamics of Hierarchy"*? We explored the intricate structures that hold organisations together, their benefits and challenges, like seasoned cartographers navigating uncharted territory. Each turn and twist revealed new insights, mapping out the complexities of organisational frameworks.

Next, we stepped into the sunlit expanse of *"openness,"* where we witnessed the transformative power of transparency. We saw how it fosters trust and cohesion within a team, just like sunlight nourishing a garden, allowing it to flourish. The rays of openness brought clarity and growth, making everything more vibrant and interconnected.

We then delved into the bedrock of *"Integrity,"* emphasising the unwavering need for alignment between actions and words. Imagine a magnificent building whose strength relies on a foundation of integrity, ensuring it withstands the tests of time. Every stone laid with honesty and consistency forms a structure that stands tall and resilient.

Our journey continued through the vibrant marketplace of *"reward and recognition,"* where fair rewards and earned recognition act as the currency that motivates and validates employees. Just like a bustling market that rewards hard work and fuels innovation, these practices create a thriving environment, buzzing with energy and creativity.

Finally, we turned our focus to the cornerstone of *"Support,"* recognising it as more than just an expense, but a powerful investment. Strong support systems foster loyalty and belonging, creating a sense of security and community within the organisation. Like the roots of a mighty tree, support anchors the organisation, allowing it to grow and weather any storm.

With these foundations in place, we are ready to journey forward, equipped with the wisdom and experiences from our past explorations. Let's continue to build, inspire and thrive together.

If we squint closely at these five elements we've discussed – hierarchy, openness, integrity, reward and recognition, and support – we'll discover a hidden gem: they all revolve around one central theme: *expectation*.

Expectations are like the threads that weave the fabric of our experiences, both as *'individuals'* and as part of a *'group.'* They shape how we perceive our work environment, influencing our satisfaction and engagement. When expectations are clear and aligned, they create a cohesive tapestry that binds us together, guiding our actions and interactions.

Hierarchy sets the stage by establishing the framework of roles and responsibilities, creating a structure where expectations are defined and understood. Openness, then, adds transparency, allowing these expectations to be communicated and adjusted as needed, fostering trust and collaboration.

Integrity ensures that these expectations are met consistently, building a foundation of reliability and trustworthiness. Reward and Recognition acknowledges when expectations are exceeded, fuelling motivation, and reinforcing positive behaviour.

Finally, Support provides the necessary resources and encouragement to meet these expectations, nurturing a culture of growth and resilience. Together, these elements form a dynamic interplay of expectations, creating a thriving and harmonious work environment.

However, the interesting fact is that each of these factors reflects the expectations we hold. Whether it's the expected hierarchy that provides structure and clarity, the expected open communication that fosters understanding and collaboration, the expected support that nurtures and empowers, the expected rewards that recognise efforts, or the expected integrity that builds trust, these elements are all anchored in our anticipations and desires.

By shedding light on these key points, we sought to address these multifaceted expectations. Understanding these dynamics is crucial because they shape the way we perceive and engage with our environment. They influence our satisfaction, our commitment, and, ultimately, our collective success.

The expected hierarchy lays down the framework, giving us a sense of order and direction. Open communication, expected and valued, paves the way for transparency and mutual respect. Support, anticipated and appreciated, strengthens our confidence and fosters a sense of belonging. Rewards, awaited and deserved, motivate us to strive for excellence. And integrity, essential and unwavering, ensures a foundation of trust and consistency.

In grasping these dynamics, we can better navigate our work environment, enhancing our satisfaction and deepening our commitment. By aligning our actions with these expectations, we not only achieve individual fulfilment, but also contribute to our collective success, creating a thriving and harmonious workplace.

While we agree that both the organisation and its people operate on a foundation of mutual expectations, it is crucial to maintain a balance between individual and organisational expectations to ensure harmony and productivity.

Thus, it was important to focus on the five factors discussed in previous chapters, which we can refer to as the 'Penta Factor' – the five pillars of a people-centric organisation.

In this chapter, we will investigate the intricate details of the *'Penta Factor'* and its surrounding elements, which encapsulate our judgements and needs. These elements are significant not only on an individual level but also collectively as a group.

When a group of individuals comes together, it must recognise and uphold all aspects of human values. However, the five core factors, known as the Penta Factor, are indispensable. These factors include hierarchy, openness, integrity, reward, and recognition, and support. They are not optional; they are essential components for any successful collaboration.

These pillars stand as the bedrock of a harmonious and productive organisation. Hierarchy provides the expected structure and clarity, guiding roles and responsibilities. Openness fosters the anticipated communication that nurtures understanding and collaboration. Integrity assures the consistency and trust we rely on. Reward and recognition acknowledge our efforts, driving motivation and excellence. Support empowers and nurtures, building a resilient and cohesive environment.

By understanding and balancing these factors, we align individual aspirations with organisational goals, creating a synergy that enhances satisfaction, commitment, and collective success. This chapter will offer a deep dive into each pillar, illuminating how they interconnect and support a thriving, people-centric organisation.

Penta Factor

In any organisation, the balance between individual and organisational expectations is crucial for harmony, productivity, and growth. The framework highlights five key elements—*Hierarchy, openness, Integrity, reward and recognition, and Support*—each playing a significant role in shaping and meeting these expectations.

At the heart of this pentagonal framework is *expectation*, representing the dynamic and reciprocal nature of the relationship between individuals and the organisation.

With the "Table of Expectations," we will explore the interplay between individual and organisational expectations across the five key elements we've discussed.

Following table will serve as a guide, illustrating how aligning these expectations can foster a balanced and mutually beneficial environment. Let's touch base on these expectations and see how they manifest in practical terms.

Table of Expectations

Element	Individual Expectations	Organisational Expectations
Hierarchy	Clear structure, support and opportunities for advancement.	Efficient decision-making, order and accountability.
Openness	Transparent information flow, voice in decisions.	Feedback engagement, collaborative problem-solving.
Integrity	Ethical behaviour, alignment of actions, and words.	Upholding values, building trust, and reputation.
Reward and Recognition	Fair acknowledgement of efforts, both monetary and non-monetary.	Motivating excellence, fostering appreciation.
Support	Resources, training, and emotional encouragement.	Enhancing skills, strategic investment in development.

For a balanced and productive work environment, it is essential to focus on three key areas:

• **Align Expectations:** Ensure that the expectations of both employees and the organisation are clearly communicated and understood. This alignment creates a shared vision and a common ground where everyone knows their roles and what is expected of them.

• **Manage Expectations:** Develop mechanisms to manage and adjust expectations as needed, addressing any gaps or mismatches proactively. This involves regular feedback and open dialogue, allowing for flexibility and responsiveness to changing circumstances.

• **Meet Expectations:** Strive to meet or exceed the expectations on both sides, fostering a culture of mutual respect and continuous improvement. By consistently delivering on promises and commitments, trust is built, and a positive, productive environment is cultivated.

Here, we need to understand what 'Expectations' truly are. It can be a feeling of anticipation, a belief that something is likely to happen, and something we think should happen.

We know the profound definition which suggests that human 'Wants' are unlimited, and this translates directly to 'Expectations', which are essentially the same as wants.

We must recognise that no one, whether an individual or a group, can meet every single expectation of everyone. Therefore, the effort must be to *meet the most expectations of the most individuals*. This approach translates into policies, procedures, and actions that are taken within an organisation.

When wants or expectations are presented to an individual or a group, they translate into choices of 'like or agreement' or 'dislike or disagreement.' It becomes a fundamental obligation to either accept or reject the choice placed before them.

However, when individuals need to act on a choice that does not meet their expectations, it triggers *cognitive dissonance.* Remember, Cognitive dissonance? It occurs when a person experiences mental discomfort or psychological stress due to holding two or more contradictory beliefs, values, or attitudes, particularly when their actions conflict with their beliefs or values. This ultimately influences both the overall organisational culture and individual well-being.

Our judgements are a powerful force, shaping both our individual and group interactions. They are informed by a rich tapestry of past experiences, interactions, and needs. To understand how we connect with our communities, it is crucial to shed light on these two fundamental factors: judgements and needs.

Judgements are influenced by a myriad of factors, including past experiences, personal values, and social interactions. They shape our perceptions and responses to various situations, affecting how we interact with others and make decisions. Judgements act as a lens through which we view the world, colouring our interpretations and guiding our actions.

Our needs and expectations are one of the powerful driving forces behind our behaviours and decisions. They encompass everything from basic physiological requirements to complex psychological desires. Understanding our needs helps us comprehend why we make certain choices and how we prioritise different aspects of our lives.

Let's reach deeper into our understanding of expectations and judgement.

The Judgement Mechanism – Matrix of Judgement

Human decision-making is a fascinating dance between reason and emotion. At the heart of this dance lies a fundamental mechanism, *The Judgement*. This model posits that we categorise the world around us, including actions, reactions, and even our understanding, through a binary lens of **"like" or "dislike."** This framework helps us understand how individuals and groups assess and react to situations based on their expectations and existing beliefs.

	Disagreement	Disagreement	
+	**Subject**	**Object**	Like
-	**Object**	**Subject**	Disike

Core Principles of the Judgement Mechanism

The Judgement Mechanism hinges on the concept of *"actions."* These actions encompass everything from spoken words to artistic expressions, encompassing the living, non-living, and even the imaginary. Our perception of these actions defines our "like" or "dislike" response. This response is further influenced by our familiarity with the action.

Actions can be categorised as "liked" (agreed to) or "disliked" (disagreed to).

Like and Dislike

- **Like-Known:** Actions readily align with our existing preferences, knowledge, or interests, leading to a natural acceptance.

- **Like-Unknown:** We encounter actions outside our current frame of reference. However, trust in the action itself, or the person performing it (the "actioner"), can still trigger a positive response.

The Flip Side of the Coin is the *'dislike'* and the Spectrum of *'disagreement.'*

Similarly, "dislike" judgements stem from actions perceived as negative. Again, familiarity plays a role:

- **Dislike-Known:** Actions clash with our established values or beliefs, leading to an immediate negative response.

- **Dislike-Unknown:** Unfamiliar actions can also trigger dislike if they appear incongruent with our expectations.

Subject and Object

The Judgement Mechanism introduces the concept of "subject" and "object." The *subject* is the initiator of the action, while the *object* is the recipient or target. The interplay between their perspectives significantly influences the outcome:

- **Positive Subject and Positive Object:** When both the initiator and recipient view the action favourably, the outcome is naturally positive (like).

- **Negative Subject or Object:** A negative perception from either the initiator or recipient can lead to (dislike).

Visualise this interaction through a simple, yet profound matrix:

Subject Perception	Object Perception	Outcome	Example
Positive (+)	Positive (+)	Like	Colleague offers to help with a project.
Negative (-)	Positive (+)	Disagreement	The manager assigns extra tasks with a dismissive tone.
Positive (+)	Negative (-)	Disagreement	Colleague asks for help, but undervalues your expertise.
Negative (-)	Negative (-)	Dislike	Boss sets unreasonable deadlines, with a controlling attitude.

Interaction is a graceful waltz. For instance, your colleague offers to help you with a complex project, leading to a mutually beneficial collaboration (like).

- **Disagreement:** Disagreements arise when there's a mismatch in perceptions. For example, if your manager assigns you extra tasks in a dismissive tone, you might complete the tasks, but the manner of assignment leaves feelings of resentment (disagreement).

- **Dislike:** When both the subject and the object hold negative perceptions, the interaction becomes a jarring cacophony. Imagine your boss imposing an unreasonable deadline with a controlling attitude, leading to decreased motivation and frustration (dislike).

Let's bring this matrix to life with a story

Sarah, a project manager, kicks off her day with a team meeting. She acknowledges her team's efforts with genuine appreciation (positive subject). The team, feeling valued (positive object), reciprocates with increased enthusiasm. This harmonious interaction sets a productive tone for the day (like).

Unexpected Assignment: The Stressful Twist

Later, Sarah receives an urgent request from her boss, Mark. He needs a report by the end of the day and communicates this in a terse email (negative subject). Sarah, already swamped with tasks, perceives this as disrespectful and overwhelming (negative object). Despite completing the report, Sarah feels undervalued and stressed (dislike).

Helping Hand: A Shift in Perception

In the afternoon, John, a senior developer, offers to assist Sarah with her workload (positive subject). Initially sceptical about John's capabilities (negative object), Sarah eventually appreciates his support as they work together. Her perception shifts positively, leading to a productive partnership ('disagreement' resolved to 'like').

By understanding the Judgement Mechanism and its matrix, you can navigate the complex dynamics of the office environment. Recognising how your perceptions and those of your colleagues influence interactions helps you foster a positive work atmosphere, manage relationships effectively, and navigate conflicts more constructively. So, the next time you face a challenging situation at work, remember this matrix and see your interactions through the lens of the Judgement Mechanism. It might just help you find your rhythm in the Monday Morning Mambo!

The Judgement Mechanism provides a framework for understanding how actions are perceived and judged within an organisational context. For an action to be liked and positively received, both the subject and the object must align positively. This alignment fosters agreement and positive judgements, which are crucial for a harmonious and productive organisational culture.

By applying The Judgement Mechanism, organisations can better navigate the complexities of human interactions and expectations, ultimately leading to a more cohesive and supportive work environment.

While the Judgement Mechanism offers a foundational framework for understanding human judgement, with the "like" and "dislike" binary providing a starting point, it's important to acknowledge the complexities of human perception.

The Judgement Mechanism offers a valuable framework for understanding perception. However, another crucial factor shapes our social interactions, particularly within organisations – *passion*. Passions are the intense desires and interests that fuel our motivation and drive. They go beyond simple needs; they represent a deeper connection, a form of "love" for a particular activity or cause.

With a foundational understanding of the Judgement Mechanism, let us delve into the concept of *passion*. Imagine a world painted in shades of "meh;" tasks feel like chores, relationships lack spark, and learning is a dull obligation. Thankfully, this isn't our reality. We all possess a powerful force that injects colour and vibrancy into our lives – passion.

Think of passion as a companion to the "Judgement Mechanism" we discussed earlier. It takes the factors we evaluate (good, bad, acceptable) and adds an emotional layer. It's like the difference between understanding the mechanics of a car and feeling the exhilaration of a joyful ride.

Just like supply and demand govern markets, passion shapes our daily interactions. When we're passionate about something – a subject, a person, an activity – it becomes a magnet drawing us in. It fuels our motivation, ignites our creativity, and even alters our perception of challenges.

Take learning, for example. A student passionate about math tackles complex problems with the same enthusiasm as a seasoned explorer approaches a new frontier. The struggle becomes a thrilling puzzle, and the solution a satisfying victory. On the other hand, a student lacking that passion might find the same problems daunting and dull.

This difference highlights the power of passion. It fosters a deeper connection, a burning desire to dig deeper, and truly understand.

The magic of passion extends to the workplace. Imagine an employee who isn't just "doing their job," but who approaches their work with genuine enthusiasm. Their passion fuels their drive to go the extra mile, not for external validation, but because the work itself brings them joy and satisfaction. This enthusiasm translates into higher productivity, better quality work, and a more positive, and contagious energy that uplifts the entire team.

Passion isn't reserved for work or hobbies; it enriches our relationships too. When we're passionate about the people in our lives, we invest more time, energy, and emotion into nurturing those bonds. This fosters deeper understanding, stronger connections, and a more fulfilling social life.

In essence, passion is the missing ingredient in the recipe for a fulfilling life. It's the emotional fuel that propels us forward, shapes our interactions, and ultimately determines how much satisfaction we derive from our pursuits. By understanding and harnessing our passions, we unlock the potential for a richer, more meaningful experience, both personally and professionally. So, the next time you encounter something – a task, a person, a new skill – ask yourself: "Does it spark a flame within?" Because the embers of passion hold the power to illuminate the most extraordinary aspects of our lives.

Theory of Passion

Our lives are a constant dance between reason and emotion. But what ignites this dance? This is where the Theory of Passion, a concept that complements the Judgement Mechanism, comes in. It hunts into three key factors influencing acceptance: ***seller, demand, and buyer***.

Imagine a marketplace where ideas, goods, or services are exchanged. The seller represents the subject matter seeking acceptance. However, unlike a traditional marketplace, the seller doesn't create demand. Instead, the demand arises from the passion or inherent importance we assign to the subject. This passion fuels our desire to engage with the seller's offering.

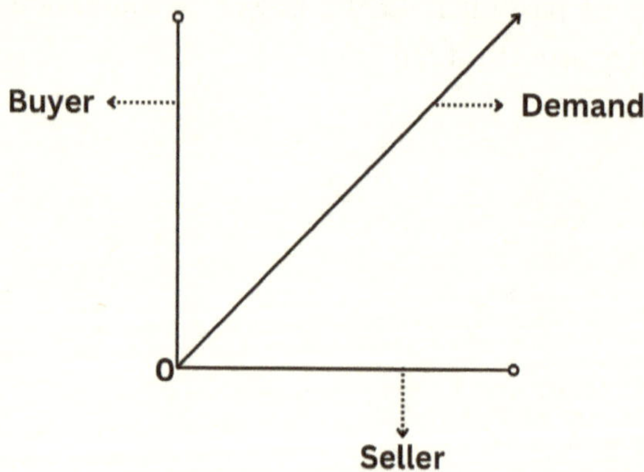

Imagine a bustling marketplace filled with ideas, products, and experiences. This marketplace represents our lives, and the sellers are all the things vying for our attention. But how do we decide what to invest our time and energy in? Here's where the Theory of Passion steps in, revealing the fascinating dance between sellers, buyers, and the power of demand.

The Sellers and The Subject

Think of the sellers as anyone or anything presenting something for us to consider – a new idea, a product, a person, even a social cause. Their goal? To capture our attention and convince us of the value of their *"subject matter."*

The Buyers and The Demand: We, the buyers, are the ultimate decision-makers. We evaluate the subject matter based on our own passions and interests – this is our *"demand."* The higher the demand, the stronger the pull we feel towards something.

For example, if we have a deep passion for music (high demand), we'll likely be more receptive to a seller offering concert tickets (high-value subject matter). But someone with no interest in music (low demand) might find those tickets completely irrelevant.

Demand isn't static; it's a dynamic interplay between two forces:

- **Intrinsic Passions:** These are our inherent desires and interests. They form the core of our demand for anything.

- **External Influences:** These are the factors that shape our perception of value. Social media trends, cultural norms, personal experiences, and even the seller's persuasiveness can all influence how important we see something.

The Decision-Making: When a seller presents a subject matter that aligns with our passions or is perceived as highly valuable due to external influences, our demand skyrockets. This, in turn, increases the likelihood of us accepting or engaging with it. Conversely, if there's little to no demand (low passion and low perceived value), the subject matter might struggle to find buyers (engagement).

Understanding our Passions

By understanding the Theory of Passion, we gain valuable insight into the forces that drive our actions and interactions. It helps us recognise how our passions shape our choices and how external influences can sway our perceptions. Ultimately, this deeper understanding empowers us to make more conscious decisions, leading to more fulfilling engagements in every aspect of life.

So, the next time we find ourselves drawn to something, take a moment to consider – is it our inherent passion guiding us, or are the external influences playing a role? This awareness allows us to step into the marketplace of life as a discerning buyer, choosing to invest our energy in things that truly resonate with our core desires.

Now the important question comes to mind: why are the Penta Factor, the concept of 'Judgement', and 'passion' so crucial?

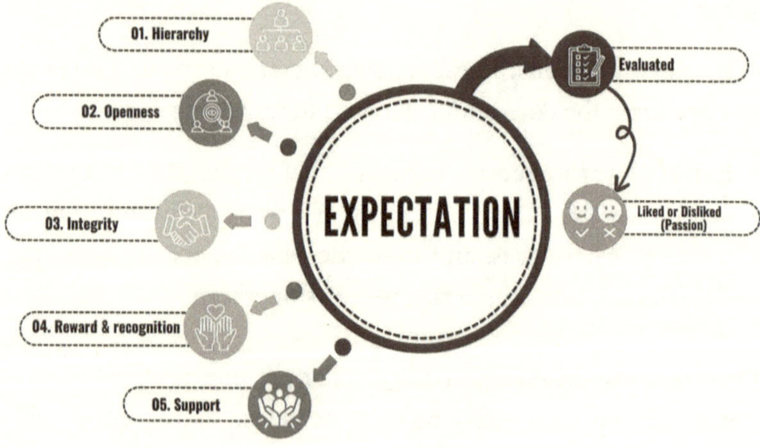

Imagine ourselves not in a towering forest, but on the cusp of a vibrant office space. Each desk, coworker, and shared coffee pot represents a unique aspect of our interactions within a team, mirroring the dynamics of a thriving ecosystem.

The Five Pillars: Building a Thriving Workplace

In this environment, the "Five Pillars" stand as the cornerstones of a successful team. These pillars are the invisible forces that shape our experiences and interactions with colleagues.

- *Hierarchy, The Towering Oak*: Structure is paramount. Just as the tall oak provides a vantage point, a clear hierarchy establishes order and interconnection. This hierarchy offers a clear line of sight, guiding direction, and maintaining balance within the team.

- *Openness: The Flowing Stream:* Information must flow freely. Openness is like a gentle stream that nourishes the soil, enabling everyone to thrive. It encourages communication and honesty, creating an environment where ideas flow freely, and every voice is heard. Transparency builds trust and fosters collaboration.

- *Integrity: The Unyielding Pine:* Integrity is the rock upon which our team relies. It provides the sturdy trunks that withstand storms, maintaining trust and stability. Like resilient pines, integrity ensures the team stands strong even in the face of challenges. It's the moral compass guiding actions and upholding commitments, fostering a culture of trust.

- *Reward and Recognition: The Wildflower Patch:* Celebrate success! Reward and Recognition are the vibrant wildflowers scattering seeds of motivation and encouragement. They acknowledge and celebrate achievements, providing the nourishment that fuels passion and drives individuals to strive for excellence. Recognition creates a positive feedback loop where effort and achievement are celebrated.

- ***Support: The Protective Canopy:*** Let's look out for one another. Support offers the protective shelter, nurturing every team member. It's the dense canopy providing shade and protection, ensuring everyone feels safe and cared for. Support fosters a sense of belonging and community, where individuals feel valued and empowered. It creates a nurturing environment where everyone can thrive and contribute their best.

- ***The Power of Judgement: Navigating the Landscape:*** As we navigate this office oasis, we constantly evaluate our surroundings. This act of judgement, like a seasoned explorer assessing the terrain, guides our path. We categorise our experiences – good or bad, supportive or dismissive – much like an explorer marking safe trails and areas to avoid. This evaluative process isn't just about survival; it's woven into the fabric of our interactions, shaping our decisions and how we connect with others.

Passion: The Lifeblood of Collaboration: Judgement breathes life into this ecosystem, igniting a powerful force – passion. Passion is the lifeblood coursing through this vibrant landscape, fuelling our actions and interactions. It transforms the office from a collection of desks into a thriving, dynamic team where each member supports and enhances the other.

Passion creates a sense of belonging and purpose, driving us to contribute our best efforts and fostering a culture of excellence. It's the invisible force binding the Five Pillars together, ensuring they not only function, but flourish.

In the world of the workplace oasis, judgement and passion are the key elements ensuring the team not only survives but thrives. They are the invisible threads weaving together the tapestry of an outstanding working environment. Here, every individual feels valued, every effort is recognised, and the collective spirit soars to new heights.

The Five Pillars, along with judgement and passion, form the recipe for a harmonious environment. It's a place where we can thrive, collaborate, and achieve excellence together. This foundation supports a thriving community where every member feels valued, supported and motivated to contribute their best.

Even within the confines of specific roles, we are fundamentally human beings. We interact with the world through a uniquely human lens, shaped by our inherent biases, desires, and personality traits. These interactions, in turn, trigger reactions from others. This intricate dance of actions and reactions shapes the very culture and environment of our organisations.

Organisations, through tools like people matrices, policies, and performance evaluations, strive to develop the workforce. However, neglecting the core factors, which we call the '*Penta Factor*', creates a void, potentially leading to unintended consequences for the organisation.

Imagine leaders wielding not just authority, but a deep understanding of the human elements that make their organisations thrive. This understanding comes from mastering the Penta Factors and every policy, and by recognising that every piece of organisational elements that interacts with people – become brushstrokes on the canvas of the organisation.

These core elements influence not just how outsiders perceive our organisation, but also how our employees feel valued. A trusted environment fosters openness, leading to a surge of passion and a deeper commitment to their work. In this symphony of trust, Integrity acts as the conductor's baton, ensuring harmony and clear direction.

Cast aside the whispers of ego. History serves as a stark reminder: the organisations that survive and flourish are those built on a foundation of collaboration. Just like a ship navigates treacherous waters through the collective strength of its crew, successful organisations rely on trust between leaders and teams.

Organisations are not factories churning out profits. True value creation starts with every individual associated with it, directly or indirectly. The Penta Factor, or any framework that prioritises the human experience, is not a revelation. Think of it as a familiar melody waiting to be rediscovered and played with renewed fervour.

The score is already written. What we need now are dedicated individuals, the conductors of their own organisations, ready to transform these principles into tangible action. The return on this human investment will be a symphony of success, far exceeding. Our journeys within the workplace are not defined solely by rigid structures, open communication, unwavering trust, well-deserved recognition, or a sense of belonging. These elements, the Five Pillars, are vital, but it's the passion we ignite and the judgement we employ that truly shapes our path. Together, they become the threads that weave a vibrant tapestry of success.

Imagine a group of individuals as a vibrant orchestra, each member playing a unique instrument. The music created is a harmonious blend of individual talents, guided by a shared purpose. This is the essence of group culture – a symphony of collaboration.

Just as in a musical ensemble, the actions of each member influence the overall performance. The ancient Indian treatise, Natya Shastra, offers a profound insight into this dynamic. It emphasises the interconnectedness of hand gestures, gaze, mind, emotion, and aesthetic experience.

While exploring this concept in the context of modern organisations, the '*Hastas*' or hand gestures represent the individual actions or efforts of each team member. These actions, influenced by the '*Drishti*' or focus, shape the overall direction of the group. The '*Manas*' or mind, representing judgement, plays a crucial role in evaluating these actions and their impact on the group's goals. The culmination of these elements is the 'bhava' or emotion, which translates to the group's overall morale and passion. And finally, the '*Rasa*' or aesthetic experience is the collective outcome, the harmonious symphony created by the interplay of individual contributions.

In essence, the Penta Factors – Hierarchy, openness, Integrity, reward and recognition, and Support – are the instruments in this grand orchestra. When played in harmony, they create a beautiful melody of collaboration and achievement. The success of the group lies not just in the individual brilliance of each member, but in their ability to play together in perfect synchronisation.

Just as a conductor guides an orchestra, effective leadership is essential in ensuring that the diverse elements of the group come together to create a harmonious performance. By fostering a culture of collaboration, trust, and respect, leaders can create an environment where every member feels valued and empowered to contribute their unique talents.

The journey towards creating a high-performing team is not without its challenges. However, by understanding the interconnectedness of individual actions and the collective impact they have on the group's success, we can navigate the complexities of modern organisations with greater clarity and purpose.

Remember, a symphony is more than just a collection of notes; it's a harmonious blend of individual talents orchestrated to create a masterpiece. So, let us strive to create workplaces where every individual is a valued musician, contributing to a symphony of success.

In this tapestry, every thread matters. A supportive email, a candid conversation fuelled by openness, or a well-timed recognition – each action strengthens the overall piece. Every voice resonates, contributing to the rich harmony of collaboration. Here, effort isn't simply acknowledged; it's celebrated, nurturing a sense of collective purpose.

The era of change is upon us. Human abilities are pushed, machines learn, and artificial intelligence emerges. Yet, amidst this transformation, one element remains constant – the enduring power of human connection. Imagine a thriving community where talents not only survive but soar. Where a legacy of excellence is built, not on individual achievements, but on the collective spirit. Here, every day becomes an opportunity – to achieve greatness together, to uplift and support one another, and to transform shared dreams into reality.

As we close this book, let's not end the journey. The greatest adventures are not confined to the pages; they unfold within the dynamic fabric of our workplace. Let's keep the music playing, one passionate interaction, one thoughtful judgement, and one resounding voice at a time, for our current understanding.

Notes

1. Nokia's Decline: The Decline and Fall of Nokia (2012) by Anssi Vanjoki et al.: This book provides a detailed account of Nokia's rise and fall, exploring the strategic decisions and internal dynamics that contributed to their decline. Why did Nokia fail and what can you learn from it? (2019) by Multiplier Magazine https://medium.com/tag/nokia: This online article offers a concise analysis of Nokia's missteps, focusing on their reluctance to embrace Android and their partnership with Microsoft.

2. https://www.britannica.com/event/Enron-scandal

3. Kodak and Polaroid Instant Cameras: Instant: The Story of Polaroid (2010) by Christopher Anderson: This book chronicles the rise and fall of Polaroid, delving into their innovative instant camera technology and their competition with Kodak.

4. How Kodak Missed the Digital Revolution (2019) by Investopedia https://www.youtube.com/watch?v=7t2uI42dY9A: This online article analyses Kodak's failure to adapt to digital photography, highlighting their focus on film and their lack of open-mindedness to new technologies. The Blockbuster Fiasco: Losing the Signal: The Untold Story of Blockbuster's Collapse (2014) by James Flint: This book investigates into the factors that led to Blockbuster's downfall, including their failure to adapt to the rise of DVD rentals and streaming services. Blockbuster's Downfall: A Cautionary Tale for Businesses (2020) by Forbes https://www.forbes.com/

sites/jonathansalembaskin/2013/11/08/the-internet-didnt-kill-blockbuster-the-company-did-it-to-itself/: This online article provides a business-oriented analysis of Blockbuster's mistakes, emphasizing the importance of adapting to changing consumer preferences.

5. The New Coke Fiasco: Marketing Mistakes and Product Flops (2001) by Stephen Brown: This book explores various marketing blunders, including the New Coke fiasco, and the importance of understanding consumer sentiment. The New Coke Debacle: A Case Study in Marketing Blunders (2023) by Harvard Business Review   https://www.coca-colacompany.com/about-us/history/new-coke-the-most-memorable-marketing-blunder-ever: This online article offers a detailed analysis of the New Coke launch and the lessons learned about consumer research and brand loyalty.

6. Rock et al., 2010, Journal of Experimental Social Psychology. Yuan et al., 2012, Communication Research.

7. Nickerson, 1998, Psychological Review

8. Project   Implicit   -   https://implicit.harvard.edu/implicit/takeatouchtestv2.html

9. Deloitte. (2021, December 7). Diversity and Inclusion. https://www2.deloitte.com/us/en/pages/about-deloitte/articles/deloitte-inclusion.html

10. Howard, F. (2003). Wilbur and Orville: A Biography of the Wright Brothers. Dover Publications.

11. Clark, M. (2018, January 11). How Kodak Missed the Digital Revolution. Harvard Business Review. https://www.hbs.edu/faculty/Pages/item.aspx?num=31757

12. Isaacson, W. (2011). Steve Jobs. Simon and Schuster.

13. https://nssdc.gsfc.nasa.gov/planetary/lunar/ap13acc.html (Apollo 13 Mission - NASA)

14. https://www.nytimes.com/2017/01/13/business/dealbook/wells-fargo-earnings-report.html

15. https://www.npr.org/series/508986161/investigating-the-wells-fargo-scandal https://www.newyorker.com/tag/elizabeth-holmes

16. https://www.max.com/movies/inventor-out-for-blood-in-silicon-valley/1d7c48f8-8064-46d7-a3b8-bb7b91fc2056 Equity Theory: Adams, J. Stacy (1963). "Toward an understanding of inequity." The Journal of Abnormal and Social Psychology 67 (4): 422–436. https://psycnet.apa.org/record/1964-04111-001

17. Social Comparison Theory: Festinger, Leon (1954). "A theory of social comparison." Human Relations 7 (2): 117–140. https://journals.sagepub.com/doi/10.1177/001872675400700202

18. Expectancy Theory: Vroom, Victor H. (1964). Work and Motivation. New York: Wiley. https://www.amazon.com/Expectancy-Theory-Literature-Jesse-Holder-ebook/dp/B08MBDHG5X

19. Attribution Theory: Heider, Fritz (1958). The Psychology of Interpersonal Relations. New York: Psychology Press. https://psycnet.apa.org/record/2004-21806-000

20. Organizational Justice: Greenberg, Jerald (1990). "Organizational justice: Fairness in the workplace." Organizational Dynamics (1): 7–27. https://psycnet.apa.org/record/2010-06019-008

21. Journal of Nursing Administration https://pubmed.ncbi.nlm.nih.gov/35186633/

22. American Association of University Women https://www.aauw.org/app/uploads/2022/08/Equal-Pay-Quick-Facts-Jan-2022.pdf

23. Google Gender Case Website: https://googlegendercase.com/ Business Today: https://www.nytimes.com/2022/06/12/business/google-discrimination-settlement-women.html https://www.dailymail.co.uk/news/article-10907613/Google-agreed-pay-118-million-settle-gender-discrimination-lawsuit.html (This article mentions the settlement amount and the nature of the lawsuit)

24. https://www.starbucksbenefits.com/en-us/home/stock-savings/bean-stock/)

25. https://www.theguardian.com/world/2020/mar/01/susan-fowler-uber-whistleblower-interview-travis-kalanick

26. https://positivepsychology.com/perma-model/

27. Graen, G. B., and Uhl-Bien, M. (1995). Relationship-based approach to leadership: Development of leader-member exchange (LMX) theory of leadership over 25 years: Applying a multi-level multi-domain perspective. The Leadership Quarterly, 6(2), 219-247.

28. Men, L. R. (2014). Strategic internal communication: Transformational leadership, communication channels, and employee satisfaction. Management Communication Quarterly, 28(2), 264-284.

29. Eisenberger, R., Stinglhamber, F., Vandenberghe, C., Sucharski, I. L., and Rhoades, L. (2002). Perceived supervisor support: Contributions to perceived organizational support and employee retention. Journal of Applied Psychology, 87(3), 565.

30. Wayne, S. J., Shore, L. M., and Liden, R. C. (1997). Perceived organizational support and leader-member exchange: A social exchange perspective. Academy of Management Journal, 40(1), 82-111.

31. https://scholarworks.utep.edu/open_etd/1938/

32. https://www.semanticscholar.org/paper/Hindsight-Bias-Roese-Vohs/e3a1affab9b875bdf9889a8f13861991d43e4eed

33. https://www.sciencedirect.com/science/article/abs/pii/0749597890900325

34. https://www.sciencedirect.com/science/article/pii/S0039368123000833

35. https://www.hbs.edu/ris/Publication%2520Files/12-096.pdf

36. https://awspntest.apa.org/search/citedBy/2000-03816-013

37. https://journals.plos.org/plosone/article?id=10.1371/journal.pone.0184733

38. Eriksson, T. S., Kovalainen, J., and Wicksteed, B. (2019). Decoupling from Moral Responsibility for CSR: Employees' Visionary Procrastination at a SME. Journal of Business Ethics, 167(2), 361-378. https://link.springer.com/article/10.1007/s10551-019-04174-z

39. Mishra, A., Mishra, A. K., and Denrell, J. (2014). Epistemic Suspicion and Strategic Decision Making: The Moderating Role of Shared Mental Models. Organization Science, 25(1), 207-226. https://onlinelibrary.wiley.com/doi/abs/10.1002/ejsp.2753

40. https://en.wikipedia.org/wiki/Rana_Plaza_collapse

www.ingramcontent.com/pod-product-compliance
Lightning Source LLC
Chambersburg PA
CBHW061346160726
47995CB00001B/193